CliffsNotes™
Exploring the
Internet with
Yahoo!®

By Camille McCue

IN THIS BOOK

- Find your way around the Yahoo! interface

- Send and receive electronic mail

- Chat with friends or celebrities

- Join online discussions of topics that interest you

- Reinforce what you learn with CliffsNotes Review

- Find more Yahoo! information in the CliffsNotes Resource Center and online at www.cliffsnotes.com

IDG Books Worldwide, Inc.
An International Data Group Company

Foster City, CA • Chicago, IL • Indianapolis, IN • New York, NY

IDG
BOOKS
WORLDWIDE

About the Author

Camille McCue, when she isn't hanging out at Yahoo!, coordinates the Ready To Learn program for the PBS affiliate in Las Vegas, Nevada, boosting children's literacy through television. She also anchors the station's technology programming, teaches educational computing at UNLV, and builds Authorware training CDs for the International Gaming Institute. Camille is also the author of *PowerPoint 2000 For Windows For Dummies* by IDG Books Worldwide, Inc.

Publisher's Acknowledgments

Editorial

Senior Project Editor: Kyle Looper
Acquisitions Editor: Steve Hayes
Copy Editor: William Barton
Technical Editors: Julie Sykes, Matt Converse

Production

Indexer: York Production Services
Proofreader: York Production Services
IDG Books Indianapolis Production Department

CliffsNotes™ Exploring the Internet with Yahoo!®
Published by
IDG Books Worldwide, Inc.
An International Data Group Company
919 E. Hillsdale Blvd.
Suite 400
Foster City, CA 94404
www.idgbooks.com (IDG Books Worldwide Web site)
www.cliffsnotes.com (CliffsNotes Web site)

Library of Congress Catalog Card No.: 99-64595
ISBN: 0-7645-8525-8
Printed in the United States of America
10 9 8 7 6 5 4 3 2 1
1O/SW/QY/ZZ/IN
Distributed in the United States by IDG Books Worldwide, Inc.
Distributed by CDG Books Canada Inc. for Canada; by Transworld Publishers Limited in the United Kingdom; by IDG Norge Books for Norway; by IDG Sweden Books for Sweden; by IDG Books Australia Publishing Corporation Pty. Ltd. for Australia and New Zealand; by TransQuest Publishers Pte Ltd. for Singapore, Malaysia, Thailand, Indonesia, and Hong Kong; by Gotop Information Inc. for Taiwan; by ICG Muse, Inc. for Japan; by Norma Comunicaciones S.A. for Colombia; by Intersoft for South Africa; by Eyrolles for France; by International Thomson Publishing for Germany, Austria and Switzerland; by Distribuidora Cuspide for Argentina; by LR International for Brazil; by Ediciones ZETA S.C.R. Ltda. for Peru; by WS Computer Publishing Corporation, Inc., for the Philippines; by Contemporanea de Ediciones for Venezuela; by Express Computer Distributors for the Caribbean and West Indies; by Micronesia Media Distributor, Inc. for Micronesia; by Grupo Editorial Norma S.A. for Guatemala; by Chips Computadoras S.A. de C.V. for Mexico; by Editorial Norma de Panama S.A. for Panama; by American Bookshops for Finland. Authorized Sales Agent: Anthony Rudkin Associates for the Middle East and North Africa.

For general information on IDG Books Worldwide's books in the U.S., please call our Consumer Customer Service department at **800-762-2974**. For reseller information, including discounts and premium sales, please call our Reseller Customer Service department at **800-434-3422**.

For information on where to purchase IDG Books Worldwide's books outside the U.S., please contact our International Sales department at 317-596-5530 or fax **317-596-5692**.

For consumer information on foreign language translations, please contact our Customer Service department at **1-800-434-3422**, fax 317-596-5692, or e-mail rights@idgbooks.com.

For information on licensing foreign or domestic rights, please phone **+1-650-655-3109**.

For sales inquiries and special prices for bulk quantities, please contact our Sales department at 650-655-3200 or write to the address above.

For information on using IDG Books Worldwide's books in the classroom or for ordering examination copies, please contact our Educational Sales department at **800-434-2086** or fax **317-596-5499**.

For press review copies, author interviews, or other publicity information, please contact our Public Relations department at **650-655-3000** or fax **650-655-3299**.

For authorization to photocopy items for corporate, personal, or educational use, please contact Copyright Clearance Center, 222 Rosewood Drive, Danvers, MA 01923, or fax **978-750-4470**.

Table of Contents

INTRODUCTION

If all the books in the world were in a vast warehouse and you were looking for a particular piece of information, you'd probably be lost unless the books were organized in a systematic way. Yahoo!'s directories provide the organization necessary to find what you seek in the vast information warehouse of the Internet.

But that's not all. Yahoo! also allows you to personalize your experience on the Web. You can read the latest headlines, keep up with stocks, use an online calendar and to-do list, and more. Add free e-mail, chats on a variety of topics, and instant messaging, and you've got a lot of features packed into a dynamic Web site!

Why Do You Need This Book?

If you can answer yes to any of the following questions:

- Do you need to learn what Yahoo! has to offer fast?
- Don't have time to read a 500 page book about the Web?
- Need to e-mail your mother before she disowns you?
- Do you need the best airfare for an upcoming vacation?

If so, then CliffsNotes *Exploring the Internet with Yahoo!* is for you!

How to Use This Book

You can read this book straight through or just look for the information you need. You can find information on a particular topic in a number of ways: You can search the index in the back of the book, locate your topic in the Table of

Contents, or read the In This Chapter list in each chapter. To reinforce your learning, check out the Review and the Resource Center at the back of the book. To help you find important information in the book, look for the following icons in the text:

This icon alerts you to something dangerous or to avoid.

This icon clues you in to helpful hints and advice.

This icon points out something worth keeping in mind.

Don't Miss Our Web Site

Keep up with the changing world of the Internet by visiting our Web site at www.cliffsnotes.com. Here's what you'll find:

■ Interactive tools that are fun and informative

■ Links to interesting Web sites

■ Additional resources to help you continue your learning.

At www.cliffsnotes.com you can even register for a new feature called CliffsNotes Daily, which offers you newsletters on a variety of topics, delivered right to your e-mail inbox each business day.

If you haven't discovered the Internet and are wondering how to get online, pick up *Getting on the Internet*, new from CliffsNotes. You'll learn just what you need to make your online connection quickly and easily. See you at www.cliffsnotes.com!

BECOMING A YAHOO!

Most people know that Yahoo! is a tool for searching the World Wide Web (many people, sadly, only go to Yahoo! when they want to find some bit of obscure Web information). But Yahoo! offers much, much more! In fact, Yahoo! offers so much to its visitors that a community has developed around the site. Members of the Yahoo! community call themselves Yahoo!s, and I'm pretty sure that you're going to want to be a Yahoo! too.

In this chapter, I tell you how to get to the Yahoo! home page, how everything works there, and how to sign up for your own Yahoo! ID and password, which is all that's necessary to join the Yahoo! community. Then, to make getting to Yahoo! even easier, I tell you how to make Yahoo! your home page. Armed with this knowledge, you're free to begin your new life as a Yahoo!.

Browsing around Yahoo!

Getting to Yahoo! is simple. Just type www.yahoo.com into your browser and press the Enter or Return key on your keyboard. When you do so, you'll see the Yahoo! home page, your gateway to exploring the vast resources of the Web.

Figure 1-1 shows the Yahoo! home page. To assist you in learning about what's available on the Internet — and how to get to it — Yahoo! set up its home page with several directories, where you can begin your exploration. You can access these directories from buttons or hypertext links (often known simply as *hyperlinks*). Clicking a hyperlink connects you to a new page that displays more information about your selection. Clicking the What's New button at the top of the Yahoo! home page, for example, opens a page listing new Web sites, headline news, and current Net Events.

Figure 1-1: Yahoo! as it appears in Internet Explorer.

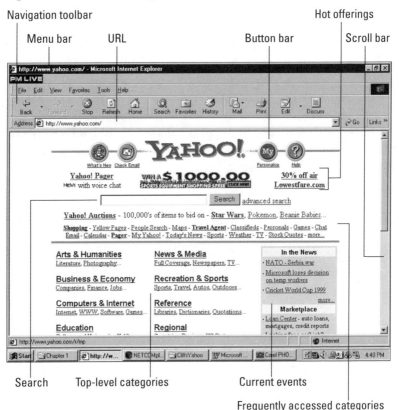

Navigation toolbar

Menu bar   URL   Button bar

Hot offerings

Scroll bar

Search   Top-level categories   Current events

Frequently accessed categories

Table 1-1 shows what each of the main areas of the Yahoo!
home page offers.

Table 1-1:   Areas in the Yahoo! Home Page

Area	What's there	What It Does
Button bar	What's New	Accesses a list of recently added Web sites, top news stories, and today's Net Events
	Check Email	Connects you with your Yahoo! mailbox
	Personalize	Connects you with My Yahoo!, your own personalized interface for using Yahoo!
	Help	Connects you with a collection of Help categories and frequently asked questions on every imaginable Yahoo! topic
Hot offerings	Hyperlinks leading to - limited-time offerings.	Changes frequently, not-to be-missed and so watch for new offerings daily
Search	A Search box	Allows you to type keywords and then search for listings in Yahoo! containing those words
Frequently accessed categories	Hyperlinks to the Yahoo! categories that experience the greatest user traffic	Provides links to such categories as Shopping, Travel, and Classifieds
Top-level categories	14 categories that organize Yahoo!'s half-million indexed Web sites into an orderly arrangement	Provides an intuitive, topic-based approach to locating information.

Continued

Table 1-1:   Areas in the Yahoo! Home Page
(*continued*)

Area	What's there	What It Does
Current Events	In the News	Presents hyperlinks to the day's latest headlines around the world
	Marketplace	Provides hyperlinks to financial issues of interest
	Inside Yahoo!	Lists two or three links to fun and frivolous Yahoo! offerings, such as movie show times in your local area
World Yahoo!s	Special international versions of Yahoo!	Present information in for a variety of countries and languageslanguages native to the areas they represent and tailor news headlines, current events, maps, and other items to those countries
Yahoo! Get Local	Yahoo! guides for your local area	Information about your local area
Other Guides	A selection of other areas of interest	Guides for buying and selling things, operating a smal l business, Y! Internet life, message boards, and the kid-friendly Yahooligans!.

Making Yahoo! Your Home Page

Whether you use Netscape Navigator or Internet Explorer as your browser, the home page is the first screen that appears each time you start your browser. Setting up Yahoo! as your home page speeds your online activities by eliminating extra steps in accessing Yahoo!. After you set Yahoo! as your home page, starting your browser starts Yahoo!, too.

In Netscape Navigator

To make Yahoo! your home page in Netscape Navigator, follow these steps:

1. Establish your Internet connection and start Navigator by doubling-clicking the Netscape program icon.

2. In Navigator, choose Edit⇨Preferences from the menu bar to open the Preferences dialog box.

3. Select the Home Page radio button, type www.yahoo.com in the Location text box, as shown in Figure 1-2, and then click OK.

Figure 1-2:   Setting up Yahoo! as your home page in Netscape Navigator.

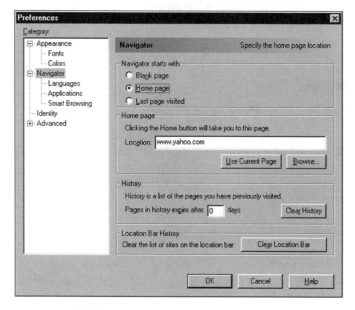

In Internet Explorer

To make Yahoo! your home page in Internet Explorer, follow these steps:

1. Establish your Internet connection and start Explorer by doubling-clicking the Explorer program icon.

2. In Explorer, choose Tools⇨Internet Options (or View⇨Internet Options in older versions) from the menu bar to open the Internet Options dialog box; click the General tab to bring it to the front if it isn't already there.

3. Type www.yahoo.com in the Address text box in the Home Page area, as shown in Figure 1-3, and click OK.

Figure 1-3: Setting up Yahoo! as your home page in Internet Explorer.

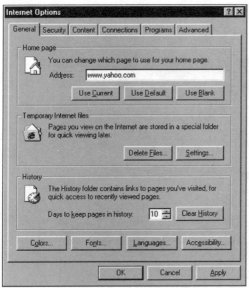

Clicking the Home button on your browser's Navigation Toolbar at any time returns you to your home page — in this case, the Yahoo! home page.

Signing Up for a Yahoo! ID

To use many of the resources at Yahoo!, you must sign up for a Yahoo! ID. Yahoo! asks you to provide this ID to enter personalized areas such as My Yahoo!, Calendar, Chat, Email, Pager and others (see Figure 1-4). You don't need an ID for general activities such as browsing or searching. Your Yahoo! ID is password-protected so that other Yahoo!s can't access your personalized areas.

Figure 1-4:   Signing up gives you access to additional Yahoo! resources.

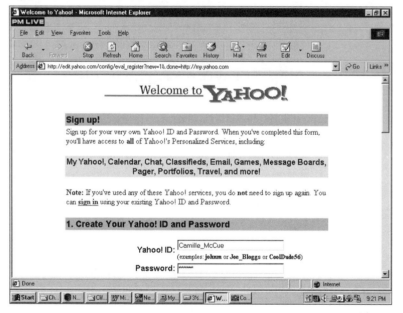

Sign up for a Yahoo! ID by using the following procedure:

1. In Yahoo!, click the Personalize button on the Button bar to access the My Yahoo! page.

2. In the Message Center, click the Get Your Own My Yahoo! hyperlink. The Sign up! page appears.

3. Complete the information on the Sign up! page by typing the appropriate information in each text box. The Yahoo! ID you choose can't include special characters or spaces, but it can contain the underscore symbol (as in Camille_McCue). Your Yahoo! ID can be a form of your name, your nickname, or something else altogether.

If Yahoo! tells you that the name you want is already in use, just add some numbers to the end until it's all yours.

Completing the Tell Us About Your Interests area is optional. Responses you give here determine what types of advertising appear at the top of each Yahoo! page. If you complete this area, Yahoo! gears the ads you see to your personal interests. Completing this area also sets up some preliminary choices for your My Yahoo! page. (See Chapter 4 for details on personalizing Yahoo!.)

4. Click the Submit this Form at the bottom of the page to submit your information to Yahoo! Alternatively, you can click the Reset this Form button to clear your entries and start over.

Yahoo! asks you to sign in using your Yahoo! ID and password whenever you attempt to enter personalized areas of Yahoo! Don't forget them!

If you forget your ID or password, click the <u>Need Help Signing In?</u> hyperlink after Yahoo! asks you to sign in. A Yahoo! Sign-In Problems page opens and asks you questions to help recall your forgotten information.

Your Yahoo! e-mail address is your Yahoo! ID with the @yahoo.com expression following it. My Yahoo! ID, for example, is Camille_McCue, so mailto:Camille_McCue @yahoo.com is my e-mail address. (See Chapter 5 for details on using Yahoo! Mail.)

CHAPTER 2
BROWSING YAHOO! CATEGORIES

IN THIS CHAPTER

- Browsing the top-14 Yahoo! categories
- Locating sites of interest
- Saving time by browsing strategically
- Bookmarking your favorite sites

One reason you probably decided to go online in the first place was to track down information on the World Wide Web. But because so many sites are out there on the Web — and because literally anyone, anywhere can create and post a Web site — finding sites that match your interests may prove as frustrating as finding specific penguins in Antarctica.

Distinguishing itself from other online information-retrieval tools, Yahoo! provides you with a directory of categories that *actual human beings* have organized into somewhere around half a million Web sites. The fact that real people make decisions about how to list its Web sites means that the Yahoo! directory presents information in a human-friendly way. Yahoo! knows, for example, that you'd look for sites referring to The Beetles under the music category — and not under insects.

Browsing Categories

Categories are the various topics into which Yahoo! organizes its information. The highest level categories are the top-level categories, which represent the broadest categories that

Yahoo! organizes information into. Each top-level category is organized into additional levels of categories. To find information on Yahoo!, you drill down into successively narrower categories.

Top-level categories

The place to begin your quest for online information is at Yahoo!'s top-level categories. Also known as the "top-14," these categories appear in big blue text, smack-dab in the middle of the Yahoo! home page at www.yahoo.com.

The top-level categories are in the middle of Yahoo!'s home page because they are, quite literally, central to the arrangement of Yahoo!. You may need to scroll down the home page to see all 14 categories simultaneously, as shown in Figure 2-1.

Figure 2-1: Top-level, or top-14 categories of the Yahoo! home page.

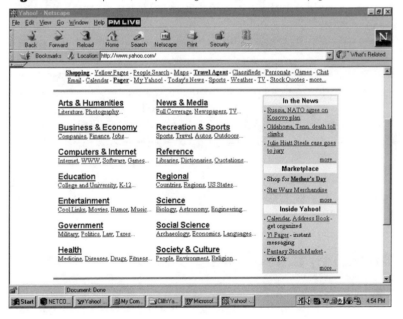

You can find every Web site that Yahoo! lists within one of these top-level categories. Notice that on the Yahoo! home page — just below each top-level category — you see a short list of some popular lower-level categories. You can see, for example, three lower-level categories under **Social Sciences**: <u>Archaeology</u>, <u>Economics</u>, and <u>Languages</u>. For the top-level category of **Health**, you see the lower-level categories of <u>Medicine</u>, <u>Diseases</u>, <u>Drugs</u>, and <u>Fitness</u>.

Lower-level categories

Each top-level category is a hyperlink to the second-level categories that make up that category. Clicking any top-level category takes you to a new page with a complete listing of all available second-level categories for that top-level listing.

If you click the top-level category of **Health**, for example, you access a list of all 20+ second-level categories under **Health**. Figure 2-2 shows how comprehensive and diverse this list is!

Following each second-level category is a number in parentheses that tells you how many third-level categories it contains. The <u>Medicine</u> second-level category of **Health** — which I refer to as **Health** ☞ <u>Medicine</u> — contains thousands of third-level categories and many of those have several lower levels of categories of their own!

Whenever the word NEW! follows the name of a Yahoo! category, you know that Yahoo! has recently added new Web sites to the subcategory.

Figure 2-2: Second-level categories under the top-level category **Health**.

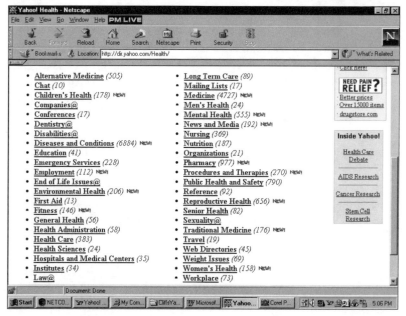

Clicking a second-level category displays a new page containing more-specific third-level categories and Web-site listings.

You can keep track of where you are within a category by looking in the upper left-hand corner of the current Yahoo! Web page. There, you see a description of your current position in Yahoo!, for example <u>Home</u> > <u>Health</u> > **First Aid**. After you click a link to a Web site, however, you temporarily exit Yahoo!, and your location within the category hierarchy no longer appears on-screen.

To backtrack and return to where you were in Yahoo!, click the Back button in your browser. Each click of the Back button backs you up by one Web page in your browser.

Browsing Strategically

Finding sites that relate to a specific subject matter that you want to explore is a skill that you can master quickly because of the logical arrangement of the Yahoo! categories. Just keep in mind that top-level categories are general and that lower-level categories become increasingly more specific. Keep in mind, too, that real people do much of the work of adding new Web sites to the Yahoo! directory every day. What that situation means to you is that other human beings are using thought processes similar to your own (well, presumably) to categorize information in Yahoo!

Yahoo! follows three simple principles for categorizing sites, which the following sections describe.

Cross-referencing

Sites can have more than one logical location in the Yahoo! categories. One person may browse for Lawyer Jokes under the top-level category of **Government**, for example, while another person may browse for the same information under **Entertainment**. To avoid duplicating information, Yahoo! assigns each site one actual "home" in the Yahoo! hierarchy and then cross-references that location from all likely pathways that users may explore to find that site.

You actually can find some great lawyer jokes, for example, by browsing Home ☞ **Government** ☞ Law ☞ Lawyer Jokes@. But Lawyer Jokes doesn't actually reside in a lower-level category of Law. The @ symbol at the end of the last category title tells you that Yahoo!'s cross-referencing you — essentially rerouting you to where you want to go. Browsing the preceding sequence routes you to where the lawyer jokes actually reside in Yahoo!, namely at Home ☞ **Entertainment** ☞ Humor, Jokes, and Fun ☞ Jokes ☞ Lawyer Jokes.

Distinguishing business sites

A firm rule that Yahoo! follows in categorizing Web sites is that business sites — regardless of what product or service the business sells — always reside in the **Business & Economy** top-level category. You may (or may not) also find these sites cross-referenced and accessible through other top-level categories keyed to the products or services that the business sells.

If you're an amateur astronomer, for example, and you're looking for a place to buy a new telescope, you can browse the following pathway: <u>Home</u> ☞ **Business and Economy** ☞ <u>Companies</u> ☞ <u>Scientific</u> ☞ <u>Astronomy</u> ☞ <u>Instruments</u>.

You can also get to the same sites, however, by browsing <u>Home</u> ☞ **Science** ☞ <u>Astronomy</u> ☞ <u>Telescopes</u> ☞ <u>Amateur</u> ☞ <u>Companies@</u>.

Don't waste time trying to find something that you want to buy by browsing categories in which you think the item itself may appear. If you know that someone, somewhere on the Web sells the item, browsing through the **Business & Economy** category ultimately expedites your search.

Distinguishing regional sites

Yahoo! simplifies the task of tracking down sites by making a distinction between those of regional interest versus sites of nonregional interest. If the sites that you seek are regional in nature, start browsing at the top-level category <u>Regional</u>. You can find art museums to visit on an upcoming trip to Barcelona, for example, by browsing <u>Home</u> ☞ **Regional** ☞ <u>Countries</u> ☞ <u>Spain</u> ☞ <u>Cities</u> ☞ <u>Barcelona@</u> ☞ <u>Entertainment and Arts</u>.

You may consider looking for museums under **Arts & Humanities**. But recognizing that museums in Barcelona are regional significantly speeds along your browsing process.

Similarly, if you're looking to join a book club in San Antonio — a regional undertaking — browse regionally under San Antonio instead of nonregionally under Book Clubs. After all, locating great book clubs in other cities doesn't do you much good!

Bookmarking Your Favorite Sites

Browsing Yahoo! should prove a fruitful process that turns up lots of Web sites matching your needs and interests. Recording the location of sites that you want to later revisit is known as *bookmarking*. Netscape Navigator refers to bookmarked sites as bookmarks, while Internet Explorers calls them favorites. To bookmark a site, follow these steps, depending on your browser:

Table 2-1:   Setting and Returning to Bookmarks

Action	*In Netscape Navigator*	*In Internet Explorer*
Setting a bookmark	Choose Window⇨ Bookmarks⇨Add Bookmark. Alternatively, from the Location Toolbar, choose Booksmarks⇨ Add Bookmark.	Choose Favorites⇨ Add to Favorites. Alternatively, from the Navigation Toolbar, select the Favorites Folder and then click the Add button.
Returning to a bookmarked site	From the Location Toolbar, choose Booksmarks and click the name of the site from the pop-up menu that appears.	From the Navigation Toolbar, choose the Favorites Folder and then click the name of the site from the favorites list.

Be aware that site addresses change frequently. A site that you bookmarked several weeks or several months earlier may no longer exist if you try to return there.

CHAPTER 3
SEARCHING YAHOO! CATEGORIES

IN THIS CHAPTER

- Searching for information by using keywords
- Reading search results
- Refining searches
- Employing other search engines

On occasions when you want to locate very precise information quickly — as opposed to casually browsing through categories — you want to use a different strategy for tracking down information online: *searching*.

Searching involves giving Yahoo! specific information for which you want it to look. Yahoo! then searches through its enormous index of categories and Web sites and tells you about everything that it finds that matches your search request. If you want, Yahoo! can even assist you in searching for information outside its categorized database, scouring the entire Web. You can then explore the matches that Yahoo! provides or refine your search criteria and search again to obtain and peruse new matches.

Searching with Keywords

A *keyword* is a word for which you ask Yahoo! to search. Keywords identify or describe the information that you want to locate online and retrieve from the Web. Typing a keyword into a search text box and clicking the Search button causes

Yahoo! to create a list for you of everywhere that word appears, not only in Yahoo!'s own categories, but also in the larger resources of the Web as a whole.

Searching by using a keyword is an especially good strategy if you know the exact name of a Web site that you want to find.

To perform a search, type a word or string of words into any search text box. Figure 3-1 shows a search from the Yahoo! home page for the University of Virginia. Notice that you don't need to use quote symbols or special formatting for the search. Just type what you want to find and click the Search button. Yahoo! returns a page of search results matching your keywords.

Figure 3-1:   Type your keywords into the search box and click the Search button to find your information.

If you typed similar keywords into the Search box at some earlier time, Yahoo! provides you with a drop-down list of all those keywords as you type. In Figure 3-1, as I type **University of**, Yahoo! reminds me that I previously searched for University of Virginia and University of Texas. You can click any search term in the drop-down list then click Search to search for those keywords.

Reading Search Results

Each time that you conduct a search, Yahoo! presents a results page providing matches for your search request. All matches returned to you are listed as hyperlinks. Clicking any category, site, or event in the list of search results connects you with the associated page, where you can further explore the information you seek.

Figure 3-2 shows the Search Results for a search on Salsa dancing. Yahoo! retrieves 1 Category Match and 33 Yahoo! Site Matches for Salsa dancing. Only the first 19 Site Matches appear on this page; scrolling to the bottom of the page provides a hyperlink that you can click to obtain the Next 14 Matches.

Figure 3-2: Search Results list matches from Yahoo! and the entire Web.

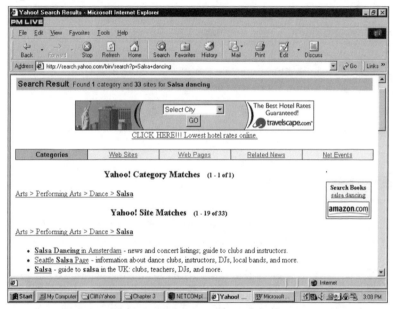

Yahoo! groups its search results into five areas, which the following sections cover.

Categories

Yahoo! Category Matches rank from the most relevant to the least relevant. The most relevant categories are exact or near exact matches for your keywords. The least relevant categories contain some of your keywords but not all. The more relevant the match is, the higher up on the results page it appears.

Each resulting category may contain thousands of related sites for you to explore. Additionally, site titles matching keywords rank higher than do matching site comments or URLs (Web addresses). A keyword search for **Beagle**, for example, ranks a site with the name *Beaglemania* higher than a site with the name *Dogmania* that only contains the word *Beagle* in its comments.

Clicking the <u>Categories</u> hyperlink at the top of the Search Results page takes you to a listing of just the matching Yahoo! Categories.

Web sites

If categories in Yahoo! match your search (called Yahoo! Category Matches), they are listed first in the search results. Individual Web sites in the Yahoo! directories that match your search are listed second (these are called Yahoo! Site Matches or Web Sites).

Web sites appear in the list along with the categories in which you find them in Yahoo!. That way, you can further explore not only the sites themselves, but also any related information in the categories in which the sites reside.

Clicking the <u>Web Sites</u> hyperlink at the top of the Search Results page takes you to a list of just the matching Yahoo! sites.

Web pages

Pages from the Web in general appear in the list only if Yahoo! can't find matches within its own resource database. If you want to find non-Yahoo! matches regardless of what Yahoo! turns up, click the <u>Web pages</u> hyperlink at the top of the Search Results page to execute a full Web search and view listings of the resulting matches.

Yahoo! doesn't actually perform the full Web search — it partners with a company called *Inktomi* that provides the search engine. Inktomi goes beyond Yahoo!'s neatly classified categories and sifts through the muck of the Web, finding everything that contains words that match some or all of your typed keywords.

Don't be surprised to see a list of hundreds or thousands of Web pages as a result of an Inktomi search!

Related News

Clicking the <u>Related News</u> hyperlink at the top of the Search Results page takes you to a listing of Yahoo! news items addressing your keyword subjects — if any exist. These news articles come from the major newspapers and television networks listed in Yahoo!'s categories.

Net Events

Clicking the <u>Net Events</u> hyperlink at the top of the Search Results page takes you to a listing of related Net Events — if any are currently scheduled with Yahoo! (See Chapter 7 for additional information on Net Events.)

Refining Searches

Sometimes Yahoo! searches with the Inktomi search engine returns more results than you really need (sometimes thousands!), with the results in the list not specifically on target. To assist you in better finding what you're seeking, Yahoo! offers an advanced search option for refining your searches. Performing an advanced search is not as daunting as it sounds — it simply requires that you complete a few areas on the Search Options page or that you learn a little bit about the language of searching (see Figure 3-3).

Figure 3-3: To refine a search, click the <u>advanced search</u> hyperlink and complete the Search Options page.

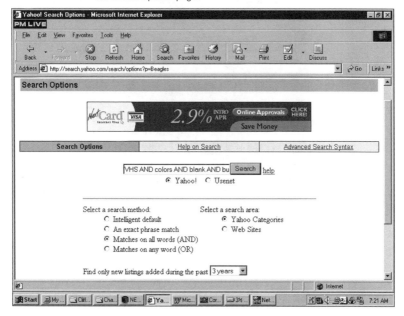

Using the Search Options page

To refine a search by using the Search Options page, click the <u>advanced search</u> hyperlink to the right of any search text box. The Search Options page opens and enables you to refine the following search parameters. To use the Search Options page, follow these steps:

1. Select either the Yahoo! radio button or the Usenet radio button. *Usenet* is a collection of Internet discussion groups that addresses information that may be current and important but doesn't necessarily rate an entire or permanent Web site. If you're looking for tidbits or very recent information, try Usenet.

With Usenet, you're getting messages that are more than likely other people's opinions — don't take something you find on Usenet as true until you've checked it thoroughly.

2. Select a search method by pressing the radio button of your choice. Yahoo! gives you the four choices shown in Table 3-1.

Table 3-1: Search Choices

Choice	What It Does	Example	What You Get
Intelligent Default	Enables you to type search keywords in natural language	**a book about Southern cooking**	Books about Southern cooking (hopefully!)
An Exact Phrase Match	Lists results that contain the exact phrase you type only	**Dallas Cowboys**	No sites about the city Dallas nor cowboys of the Old West — only about the football team
Matches on All Words (AND)	Finds every keyword that you type in a site to list it	**Meg Ryan Tom Hanks movie**	A list of sites about the movies *Sleepless in Seattle* and *You've Got Mail* but none about *Big* or *When Harry Met Sally.*
Matches on any word (OR)	A match on any keyword that you type causes Yahoo! to list a site	**Meg Ryan**	Sites containing at least one of her names; sites about Meg (including other people named Meg); sites about Ryan (including sites about *Saving Private Ryan* and *Ryan's Hope*); and sites about Meg Ryan.

3. Select either the Yahoo! Categories radio button to search within Yahoo!; or the Web Sites radio button to search the entire Web.

4. Click the down arrow next to the Find Only New List-ings Added During the Past drop-down list box to choose a time frame for how recent you want the listings to be. Choices range from one day to three years.

5. Click the down arrow next to the Number of Matches Per Page drop-down list box to choose how many match-ing results you want to appear on each page following the first page. Choices range from 10 to 100 matches. (**Note:** You may have to scroll down to find this list box as it is located at the bottom of the Search Options page.)

Click the <u>search tips</u> hyperlink at the bottom of the Search Options page for additional clues on refining your searches.

Supplying search syntax

Another alternative for refining your search (without open-ing the Search Options page) is to type your keywords using a special search language or search syntax. *Search syntax* refers to the way that you connect the words you type into the Search text box. Table 3-2 includes some simple search-syn-tax tips for helping refine your search.

Table 3-2: Search Syntax Tips

Action	What It Does	Typing This	Returns This
Place keyword phrases in quotes	Returns only sites that contain an exact match of the phrase in quotes	**"Air Force One"**	Only sites about Air Force One — not sites about the Air Force, the air, or the Force (as in, *May the Force be with you*).

Continued

Table 3-2:   Supplying search syntax (*continued*)

Action	What It Does	Typing This	Returns This
Type a + sign in front of a word	Ensures that the word following the + sign appears on the Web pages returned.	**Tyranno-saurus + Barney**	Only sites that contain the word *Barney* in the results list. These sites may or may not contain *Tyrannosaurus*.
Type a – sign in front of a word	Returns only sites that don't include the word following the – sign	**Tyranno-saurus – Barney**	No site containing the word *Barney* will appear in the list of results. The sites may or may not contain *Tyrannosaurus*.
Combine quotes, + signs, and – signs	Combines the uses of each of the syntaxes together in the same search	**"Air Force One" –movie +president**	Only sites about the actual U.S. president's airplane and not those about the movie starring Harrison Ford.

Employing Other Search Engines

Other search tools besides Yahoo! and Inktomi are available for you to use in tracking down sites. These search tools are known as *search engines*, and — as is true of Inktomi — their job is to scour the entire Web and return to you matches based on keywords that you supply. Common search engines include *Alta Vista, HotBot, Infoseek,* and *Lycos.* Any time that you perform a search, Yahoo! gives you the option of extending your search by clicking any of these additional search engines, as shown in Figure 3-4.

Figure 3-4:   Links to Other Search Engines offer you additional search results.

Other Search Engines
Alta Vista - HotBot - Infoseek - deja.com - Lycos - More...

CHAPTER 4
PERSONALIZING YAHOO! WITH MY YAHOO!

IN THIS CHAPTER

- Signing in and out of My Yahoo!
- Getting cozy with the My Yahoo! interface
- Personalizing My Yahoo! to fit your interests and style

One of the most exciting things about going online is that — unlike watching television — you can choose the stories and information you want to view. You can save a lot of time, because you don't have to sift through information that doesn't interest you!

Yahoo! provides a handy tool that performs the legwork for you in gathering and presenting information customized to your own needs. It's called My Yahoo!, and with it you can assemble a unique collage of information that's updated and displayed daily on your own special Web page. Now, instead of watching the Weather Channel, reading the newspaper and calling the airlines to check travel fares, just log into My Yahoo! and have that information delivered to you in a single location! In this chapter, you learn everything you need to know about personalizing My Yahoo! to your own interests.

Getting into My Yahoo!

To set up and use your personalized Web pages, you must first access My Yahoo!. While working in Yahoo! (www.yahoo.com), you can summon My Yahoo! in three ways:

■ Click Personalize button (the My button) in the Button bar.

■ Click the <u>My Yahoo!</u> hyperlink listed among the Frequently Accessed Categories area on the Yahoo! home page.

■ Type `http://my.yahoo.com` in the Location area of your browser and press Enter or Return.

Each time you access My Yahoo!, you have to sign in so that Yahoo! can display your personalized pages according to your unique preferences. In the Message Center on the left side of My Yahoo!, sign in by typing your Yahoo! ID and password and clicking the Sign In button.

Click the Remember my ID & Password check box to bypass the sign-in process in the future.

The first time you sign in to My Yahoo!, Yahoo! constructs your first personalized page (My Front Page) from the interests you supply after signing up for your ID and Password. (See Chapter 1 for details on Signing Up to get a Yahoo! ID and password.) For instance, if you indicate an interest in computers and technology, My Yahoo! initially sets up a My Front Page containing new technology headlines.

If you don't like My Yahoo!'s choices, don't fret! You can easily recustomize your pages at any time. Check out "Personalizing Pages in My Yahoo!" for help on setting up custom content on each of your pages.

Looking at My Yahoo!

Take a moment to meet My Yahoo!, because chances are good that it will remain a friend for a long time. The My Yahoo! interface contains several tabs, each of which represents a distinct, personalized page of information. Information on each page — such as Weather or TV Listings — appears in small chunks called modules, which are arranged into columns.

Your first personalized page is named My Front Page, as shown in Figure 4-1. This page is comprised of modules related to choices you made during sign in. If you said you had an interest in Entertainment during sign-in, you probably have modules for Television or Movie Listings located on My Front Page. Later in the "Selecting content modules" section, you learn how to change the name of My Front Page and how to change which modules appear along with the layout and color scheme of the page.

Figure 4-1:   Some important elements on My Front Page.

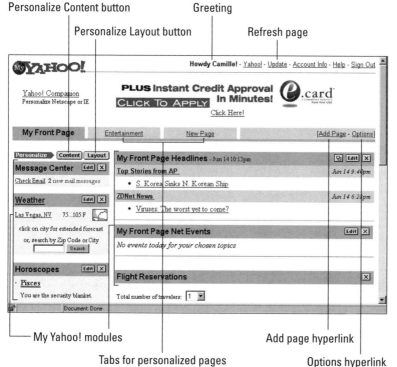

Personalize Content button

Personalize Layout button

Greeting

Refresh page

My Yahoo! modules

Tabs for personalized pages

Add page hyperlink

Options hyperlink

Adding Pages in My Yahoo!

Besides My Front Page, you can add additional pages (up to six total), each personalized for your unique interests and information that you want to track online. For example, you may want to maintain a page for sports, a page for your craft or hobby, and a page for news. You can access each personalized page by pressing its associated tab in My Yahoo!.

Follow these steps to create a new personalized page:

1. At My Yahoo!, click the Add Page hyperlink. The Create a New Page page appears, as shown in Figure 4-2.

Figure 4-2: Creating a new page in My Yahoo!.

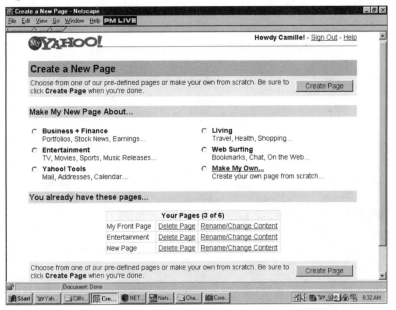

2. Select the radio button that reflects your interest in the Make My New Page About area. You can include pages about business and finance, entertainment, special Yahoo! tools, and so on.

3. If you selected any radio button except the Make My Own button, then click the Create Page button to add your new page.

4. If you selected the Make My Own radio button in Step 2, then you go instead to the Personalize Page Content for New Page page where you choose what you want to appear on your page. Click the Change Layout button to tweak the arrangement of your chosen modules on your new page. Click the Finished button to complete the addition of your Make My Own page.

Yahoo! returns you to the My Yahoo! page where you can now see a tab for your new page. Congratulations! You've successfully added a new content page.

Personalizing Pages in My Yahoo!

A great thing about My Yahoo! is that you can adapt it to your personal tastes. If you clicking the tab of the page you want to edit and then you can personalize pages in three ways:

- **Content button:** Clicking this button leads you to pages that offer you control over what information is presented on your My Yahoo! page. More than 60 modules are available for you to customize your page. The modules are arranged into easy-to-understand categories, such as My Yahoo! Business & Finance and News & Weather.

- **Layout button:** Clicking this button accesses pages that allow you to change the arrangement of modules on a personalized page. For instance, you can use Layout to put the most important modules near the top of your personalized pages.

Selecting content modules

To select which information modules appear on one of your My Yahoo! personalized pages, follow these steps:

1. In My Yahoo!, click the tab of the page on which you want to edit content modules. For this example, click the My Front Page tab.

2. Press the Content button in the Personalize area. This summons the Personalize Page Content for My Front Page page, as shown in Figure 4-3.

Figure 4-3:   Choosing modules for My Front Page.

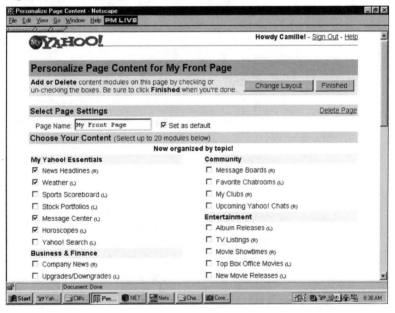

3. In the Select Page Settings area, type a name in the Page name box. My Front Page can be anything you want to call it, but for this example, leave the name as My Front Page.

4. In the Choose Your Content area, click the check boxes to select the modules you want displayed on your page. (You can choose up to 20 modules.) Clicking to uncheck a box removes that module from your page.

Remember

Each module is designated as either a left-hand side module (noted by the letter *L*) or a right-hand side module (noted by the letter *R*). Left-hand side modules are narrow, occupying about one-third of the page. Right-hand side modules are wide, occupying about two-thirds of the page.

5. Press the Finished button to complete the content personalization and return to My Front Page. The page now includes your modules.

Personalizing content

Modules that contain a small Edit button can be custom-tailored to present precisely the content you want to view. For example, clicking the Edit button on the My Front Page Headlines module summons a page (named Choose Your Headlines for My Front Page) listing Available Sections from which you can select your headline topics.

Clicking any of these Available Sections, such as Current Events & Politics, summons another page listing the news resources available to you. These news resources, such as Top Stories from AP, are listed in the Available Sections area, as shown in Figure 4-4.

Figure 4-4: Choose your headlines from the Available Sections area.

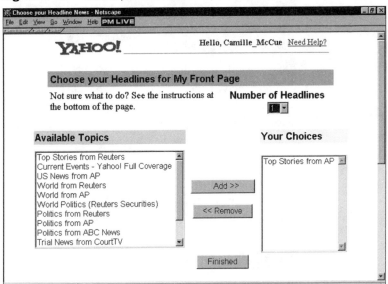

Here's how to select a topic (or other resource) to display in your module:

1. Click the name of the topic in Available Topics and click the Add button. Doing so moves the topic to the Your Choices column.

2. Remove a topic by selecting it in the Your Choices list and clicking the Remove button. Doing so moves the topic back to the Available Topics column.

3. Click the arrow in the Number of Headlines box and select from the drop-down list how many headlines you want displayed for each resource.

4. Click the Finished button to accept your choices and close the page of Available Topics. Yahoo! returns you to the page of Available Sections.

5. Click the Finished button again to return to My Front Page. The module you worked on in My Front Page now reflects your edits.

Personalizing layout

After you select modules for display on a personalized page, you have the option of rearranging their layout. To set up the layout of a page in My Yahoo!, follow these steps:

1. In My Yahoo!, click the tab of the page you want to edit. For example, click the My Front Page tab.

2. Click the Layout button in the Personalize area to summon the Personalize Page Layout for My Front Page page, as shown in Figure 4-5.

Figure 4-5: Setting up your page layout.

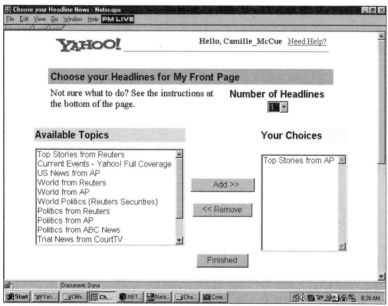

3. In the Change Layout area, your selected content modules appear listed in the Left Side or Right Side areas. Modules are listed top to bottom, in the order of their physical page layout. You can adjust the layout of modules on your page as shown in Table 4-1.

Table 4-1: Module Customization Procedures

To Do This	Do This
Move a module up	Select the name of the module and then click the up-arrow button. Each click moves the module up one position in the layout.
Move a module down	Select the name of the module and then click the down-arrow button. Each click moves the module down one position in the layout.
Delete a module	Click the name of the module and then click the × button. A warning message appears stating that you are about to delete the selected module. To proceed with deleting the module, click OK; click Cancel to keep the module.

4. Click the Finished button to complete the layout and return to your page. The My Yahoo! page now displays your new layout.

Deleting Pages in My Yahoo!

Getting rid of a personalized page you no longer want is even easier than adding a page. To eliminate a personalized page, follow these steps:

1. At My Yahoo!, click the tab representing the page you want to delete.

2. Click the Content button in the Personalize area. Doing so summons the Personalize Page Content for your chosen page.

3. Under Select Page Settings, click the <u>Delete</u> hyperlink. A warning page appears, asking if you're sure you want to remove the page.

4. Click the <u>Yes</u> hyperlink to delete the page, or click the <u>No</u> hyperlink to keep the page.

Signing Out

If you're sharing a computer with another Yahoo! user, you may both want to access your own individual My Yahoo! pages. For multiple persons to use My Yahoo! from the same computer, one person must sign out of My Yahoo! before another person can sign in.

To sign out of My Yahoo!, just click the <u>Sign Out</u> hyperlink at the top of the My Yahoo! page. A Thank You for Using My Yahoo! page appears, letting you know you've successfully signed out. This page also contains a <u>Return to My Yahoo!</u> hyperlink that returns to the My Yahoo! page so that a different user can sign in and access his or her own personalized pages.

CHAPTER 5
KEEPING IN TOUCH WITH YAHOO! MAIL

IN THIS CHAPTER

- Signing in to Yahoo! mail
- Touring the mailroom
- Sending e-mail
- Reading e-mail
- Setting up your address book
- Organizing e-mail in folders

Correspondence has come a long way in the last hundred years. From painting with quill and ink on papyrus to typing on letterhead, no writing method has been easier than word processing on a computer. And no delivery method has been faster than sending your computer correspondence at the speed of the Internet. Electronic mail, or e-mail, helps you keep in touch with friends, relatives, and colleagues — anyone you may previously have written a letter to.

Yahoo! Mail provides you with a free, easy-to-use e-mail service that connects you with every other e-mail user on the planet. If you have Internet access and a browser then you can sign in to Yahoo! and check your e-mail from any computer in the world. With Mail, you can compose and send e-mail, read arriving e-mail, and even maintain an address book of contacts with whom you correspond. Instead of checking the white wooden box for mail, you'll soon be logging in to read e-mail delivered to your Yahoo! Inbox.

Signing In to Yahoo! Mail

Yahoo! Mail is just one click away from the Yahoo! home page. Access Mail using one of the following methods:

■ At the Yahoo! home page (www.yahoo.com), click the Check Email button.

■ At the Yahoo! home page (www.yahoo.com), click the Email hyperlink in the Frequently Accessed Categories area at the top of the page.

■ Type http://mail.yahoo.com into your browser and press Enter or Return.

You have to be signed in with your Yahoo! ID and password to access Yahoo! Mail. I tell you how to attain an ID and password in Chapter 1.

After you sign in, Yahoo! presents you with the Mail home page, as shown in Figure 5-1. Here, you see several information areas, the most important of which are the Unread Messages area and the Mail menu. The Unread Messages area tells you how many new messages you have waiting in your Inbox.

Clicking the Inbox hyperlink in this area performs the same task as clicking the Check Mail hyperlink in the Mail area.

Working with the Address Book

The Address Book is a place where you can store names, e-mail addresses, and phone numbers of persons with whom you correspond via Yahoo! Mail. You can summon the Address Book, as shown in Figure 5-2, by clicking the Addresses hyperlink in the Mail menu. The friends and acquaintances in your address book are known as contacts.

Figure 5-1: The Mail home page.

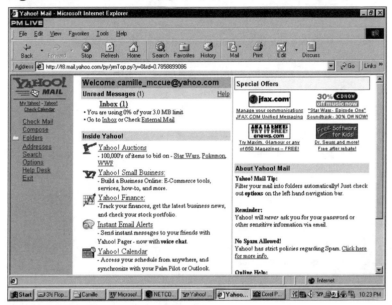

Figure 5-2: Store names, e-mail addresses, and other contact information in the Address Book.

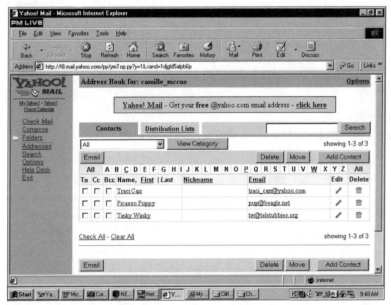

Adding new contacts

The first time you open Mail, you won't have any contacts listed. Mail gives you the following message: Welcome to your Address Book. Your address book is currently empty. To begin adding people, click above on the Add New Contact button.

To add a new contact, follow these steps:

1. Click the Contacts tab of the Address Book and then click the Add Contact button. The New Address Book Entry page appears.

2. Complete the empty boxes in the Enter New Information area. Be sure to complete the First name, Last name, and Email boxes.

3. To include more detailed information about the contact, click the Add More Detail button and add other information that you want to remember about the contact.

4. Click Done to add the contact to your Address Book. Added contacts are listed beneath the A–Z tabs in the Address Book.

You can also add the sender of any e-mail as a new contact in your Address Book. To do so, click the Add to Address Book hyperlink after reading the sender's message in your Yahoo! Mail Inbox.

Editing, deleting, and sorting contacts

At any time, you can edit information for an existing contact, delete a contact, or sort contacts:

■ **To edit a contact:** At the Contacts tab of the Address Book, click the Pencil icon located on the same line as the contact you want to edit.

■ **To delete a contact:** At the Contacts tab of the Address Book, click the Trash Can icon located on the same line as the contact you want to delete.

■ **To sort contacts:** At the Contacts tab, choose to sort alphabetically by the contact's first name, last name, nickname, or e-mail address. To sort on any of these options, simply click the hyperlink for that option. For example, clicking the <u>Last</u> hyperlink causes all contacts to be alphabetized by their last names.

The A–Z tabs in the Address Book show hyperlinks for all letters representing the last names of contacts. For instance, an entry of the last name Winky causes the W tab to become a hyperlink. Clicking a letter's hyperlink causes the Address Book to list all entries for that letter.

Composing and Sending E-mail

To write an e-mail in Yahoo! Mail, you must access the Compose Mail page by clicking the <u>Compose</u> hyperlink in the Mail menu of the Yahoo! Mail main page. Figure 5-3 shows the Compose Mail page with an e-mail in progress.

Figure 5-3: Type a message, select a recipient, and click Send.

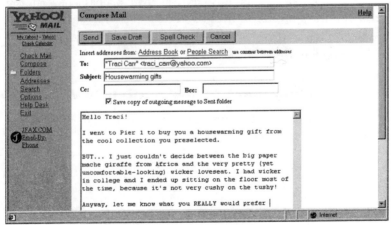

To compose and send an e-mail, just follow these steps:

1. In the To area, type the e-mail address of the recipient. Separate multiple recipients by commas. If the recipient is a contact in your Address Book, click the Address Book hyperlink, and in the Address Book, select the To check box next to the recipient's name, and then click Done.

2. In the Subject box, type a subject (or *very* brief description of what you're writing about) for the e-mail.

3. In the Cc (carbon copy) area, type the e-mail addresses of any additional people to whom you want to send a copy of the e-mail. Separate multiple recipients by commas. Recipients see who is listed in the Cc list.

4. In the Bcc (blind carbon copy) area, type the e-mail addresses of any additional people to whom you want to send a copy of the e-mail. Separate multiple recipients by commas. Recipients do *not* see who is listed in the Bcc list.

5. If you want, select the Save Copy of Outgoing Message to Sent Folder check box. Doing so enables you to maintain a duplicate record of the e-mail you send.

6. Type your message in the large blank box. Typing text that extends beyond the bottom edge of the box causes a scroll bar to appear on the right side of the box.

7. If you have documents that you want to attach to your e-mail, click the Edit Attachments button at the bottom of the e-mail. Click the Browse button to locate the file you want to send with your e-mail and then click the Attach This File button. You can attach up to three files, but the combined size of the attachments can't exceed 1.5MB. Click the Done button after you're finished attaching files.

If you want, click the Spell Check button to check for spelling errors in your e-mail.

8. Click the Send button to send your e-mail. Yahoo! Mail issues a message letting you know that your e-mail has been sent.

If you're interrupted while composing your e-mail, you can save your work without sending or losing what you've already typed. Just click the Save Draft button — before signing out — to save the unfinished e-mail in the Drafts folder. Your e-mail is saved but not sent.

Like regular mail, you can't take back an e-mail after you send it. Think hard before clicking Send on a "nastygram" e-mail!

Reading Received E-mail

To read new messages in Yahoo! Mail, click the Inbox or Check Mail hyperlink on the Mail main page, which opens your Inbox, as shown in Figure 5-4. You see new messages listed there after they first arrive. Click the Subject of any message to open the Read message page on which you can view the message's contents.

Figure 5-4   New e-mail messages arrive in your Mail Inbox.

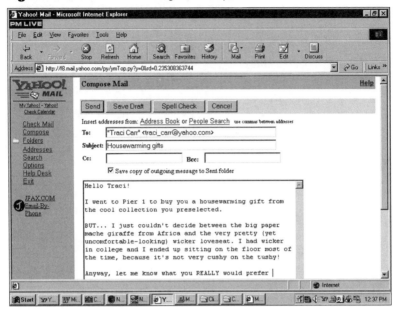

Table 5-1 lists some things that you can do after reading a new message.

Table 5-1:   What to Do with Your Message

If You Want To. . . .	*. . .Then Do This*
Delete the message	Click the Delete button to delete the message from your Inbox. This action moves the message to the Trash folder, where it stays until you empty the Trash.
Move a message to another folder	Click the arrow at the Choose a Folder drop-down list, and choose a folder to where you want to move the message. Click the Move button to complete the move.
Download attachments	Click the Download Attachments hyperlink to download and open documents that have been delivered with the e-mail.

Continued

Table 5-1: What to Do with Your Message
           (continued)

If You Want To. . . .	. . .Then Do This
Reply to the message	Click the Reply button to reply to the sender of the message. Click the Reply to All button to reply to every person who received the e-mail, including Cc and Bcc recipients.
Forward the message	Select either as an attachment or as inline text and click the Forward button to send the current e-mail to someone else.
Read a different message	Click the Prev hyperlink to read the previous message in the Inbox. Click the Next hyperlink to read the next message.
Return to the Inbox	Click the Back to Inbox hyperlink to return to the Inbox.

Organizing E-mail in Folders

To keep e-mail organized in your mailbox, Yahoo! Mail provides you several mail folders, along with the option of creating additional, customized folders. Using folders enables
you to group related e-mail together so that you can easily
locate sent and received e-mail based on its subject matter or
its sender.

You can access Folders by clicking the Folders hyperlink in
the Mail menu of the Yahoo! Mail main page. Table 5-2
shows some of the tasks you can perform while in Folders.

Table 5-2: Things You Can Do with Folders

To Do This	Do This
View folder statistics	All currently existing folders are listed in the Folder column. For each folder, the total number of messages and the number of unread messages in the folder is also listed.

To Do This	Do This
Open a folder	Click the hyperlink name of a folder to open the folder. A listing of all messages in the folder appears.
Read a message in an open folder	Click the hyperlinked subject of any message to read it.
Delete a message from a folder	Click in the check box next to the message you want to delete, and then click the Delete button.
Delete all messages in the Trash Can	Click the <u>Empty</u> hyperlink in the Folders column.
Create a personal folder	In the Create a Personal Folder area, type the name of a new folder, and then click the Create new folder button. The new folder appears in the Folders column.
Edit a folder	In the Edit a Personal Folder area, click the arrow and select a folder from the drop-down list. To rename the folder, click the Rename button, type in a new name in the pop-up window, and click OK.
Delete a folder	In the Edit a Personal Folder area, click the arrow and select a folder from the drop-down list; then press the Delete key. (**Note:** Only empty folders can be deleted.)

CHAPTER 6
JOINING THE YAHOO! COMMUNITY

IN THIS CHAPTER

- Joining online clubs
- Playing Yahoo! games
- Checking the weather
- Getting directions
- Helping youngsters access Yahooligans!

Yahoo! is the neighborhood of the '90s. It consists of a culturally diverse cross-section of people who share the common interest of going online. It's a place where people meet each other, post and read notes on community message boards, and swap ideas in virtual clubs. It's a place where folks — young and old, friendly and grouchy — play a Saturday-afternoon game, eavesdrop on neighborhood gossip, and find out about the weather.

Best of all, the people who make up the Yahoo! community — "Yahoo!s," as they're known — don't necessarily live anywhere near one another. That's because Yahoo! brings together people from all around the world — and not with cars, ships and airplanes but with computers, modems, and the Yahoo! interface to the World Wide Web. As an added bonus, the Yahoo! neighborhood is completely free from barking dogs! It's a place where Mr. Rogers could proudly say, "Won't you be my neighbor?"

Joining a Club

Yahoo!'s collection of online clubs provides gathering places for people with specific interests or hobbies to meet and discuss their ideas. From Wrestling enthusiasts to Beanie Baby collectors, you can find Yahoo!s — just like you — who've created clubs dedicated to their "weekend warrior" activities. Use either of the following methods to access Yahoo! Clubs:

- At the Yahoo! home page (at www.yahoo.com), click the more . . . hyperlink in the Frequently Accessed Categories area at the top of the page; then click the Clubs hyperlink.

- Type http://clubs.yahoo.com into your browser and press Enter or Return.

On the Yahoo! Clubs page, you can find several areas that can help you become an active club participant. Table 6-1 provides a quick synopsis of what the four most important areas do.

Table 6-1:   Important Areas on the Yahoo! Clubs Page

Area	Do This	To Do This
Search Clubs	Type an interest, such as **Star Trek** or **Toenail Art**, into the text box and click the Search Clubs button	View a list of specific clubs related to your interest
Clubs Directory	Click a top-level club category	View a list of lower-level categories of clubs under that overall category
	Click a hyperlinked club name	Browse through the club charter and the messages exchanged in the club.

Continued

Table 6-1: Important Areas on the Yahoo!
(*continued*)

Area	Do This	To Do This
	Click the Create a Club button	Create a new club.
Club Page	Click the <u>Join this Club</u> hyperlink and fill out the form that appears	Join that club
	Click the <u>post</u> hyperlink	Post a message to the club (must be a member of the club)
	Click the <u>view all</u> hyperlink	View a list of all messages posted to the group
My Clubs	Click a hyperlink to a club in the list	Go to that club

Posting and Reading Messages on Message Boards

Yahoo! Message Boards enable people to post and read messages addressing a wide variety of topics. They function similarly to Chat Rooms except that participating Yahoo!s don't all need to be present simultaneously to air their ideas — or read those of others. You can post a message at any time and return later to see what messages are posted in response to your comment, questing, or musing. Message board "conversations" can include hundreds of postings for a single topic or theme. Use either of the following methods to access Yahoo! Message Boards:

■ From the Yahoo! home page (at www.yahoo.com), choose the <u>Message Boards</u> hyperlink from the Other Guides area at the bottom of the page.

■ Type http://messages.yahoo.com in your browser and press Enter or Return.

You must sign in to Yahoo! before posting messages to the Message Boards.

A Message Board is available for each of the following categories: Business & Finance, Computers & Internet, Current Events, Entertainment & Arts, Health, Society & Culture, Sports & Recreation, and U.S. States. Each of these main Message Board categories contains several lower-level categories. Each lower-level category contains sequentially posted messages for a variety of discussion topics. Figure 6-1 shows a message posting for an ongoing discussion in the lower-level Books & Literature category of the primary Entertainment & Arts category.

Figure 6-1:   A posting to a Message Board.

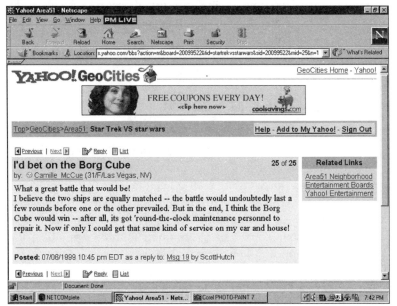

The subject of each message on a Message Board appears as a hyperlink. Click the subject hyperlink to read its associated message. Each message also lists its writer as a hyperlink, and you can click the writer's name to view a Yahoo! Profile for that person. You can scroll backward and forward through the posted messages in an ongoing discussion by clicking the Previous and Next buttons at the top of the message, or you can return to the entire list of messages by clicking the List hyperlink. Click the Reply hyperlink to post your own message and add your comments to the dialogue.

The first time that you click the Reply hyperlink, Yahoo! performs a simple procedure to verify your identity and account information before you can post messages on the Message Boards. Just follow the directions that appear on-screen and heed the warning not to post advertisements or use offensive or harassing language on the Message Boards.

If you post advertisements or use offensive language on the Message Boards, your sign-in privileges will be withdrawn — which will prevent you not only from using the Message Board but from using any personalized features of Yahoo!

Playing a Game at Yahoo!

Yahoo! Games is a playing field where both the competitive and not-so-competitive Yahoo!s can gather to play. Games presents an assortment of solo and multi-player games that you can play online with other Yahoo!s. To participate in Yahoo! Games, your browser must be capable of running Java applets — meaning that you need Internet Explorer 3.0 or Netscape 3.0 or higher. Summon Yahoo! Games by using either of the following methods:

- At the Yahoo! home page (at www.yahoo.com), click the Games hyperlink in the Frequently Accessed Categories area at the top of the page.

- Type http://games.yahoo.com in your browser and press Enter or Return.

Many games offer the option of participating as an observer, so you can watch the action just for fun or to learn new games with which you're not familiar. You can even host your own game and invite others to come and play! Whether playing or observing, you can chat with other players in the room in much the same way that you talk with other people during a "real-live" game.

Table 6-2 describes the various Yahoo! Games areas that you can explore.

Table 6-2:   Yahoo! Game Areas

Area	*Subarea*	*What You'll Find*
Games		Online, Java-delivered games that you can play and observe.
	Board Games	Backgammon, Checkers, Chess, Go, Reversi
	Word Games	Single-player Crossword
	Fantasy Games	Women's World Cup Pick 'em Contest, Fantasy Soccer, Fantasy Baseball, Stock Market Challenge
	Card Games	Blackjack, Bridge, Cribbage, Euchre, Gin, Hearts, Pinochle, Poker, Sheepshead, Spades
	Tile Games	Mah Jong
Reviews & News		The latest downloadable game demos and game-playing tips for Mac, Windows, Nintendo, and PlayStation platforms.
Communities		Game clubs where you can discuss games, get player ratings, and enter tournaments. This area also informs you of upcoming Net Event games.

On a Friday or Saturday night, you can find upward of 10,000 people playing Yahoo! Games, observing game play, and chatting with one another. You can always find someone ready and willing to play a game with you!

If another player harasses you during the game, you can filter out that person's messages. Just select his or her name in the list of players and then click in the Ignore check box in the Player Information window that appears.

Getting the Weather

Wondering about the weather was probably one of the earliest topics of neighborly conversation. Today, Yahoo! leaves you little to wonder about, because it provides you with the most up-to-date weather information from all around the world, using the most technologically advanced instrumentation available. Summon Yahoo! Weather page by using one of the following methods:

■ From the Yahoo! home page (at www.yahoo.com), click the <u>Weather</u> hyperlink in the Frequently Accessed Categories area at the top of the page.

■ Type http://weather.yahoo.com in your browser and press Enter or Return.

At the main Yahoo! Weather page, you get the following two options for finding out about the weather anywhere in the world:

■ **Search by Zip Code or City:** Type the Zip code or the name of the city — for example, **89109** or **Las Vegas** — where you want to check the weather. This search is shown in Figure 6-2.

- **Browse to Locate a City:** Click the hyperlink name of a continent, such as <u>Antarctica</u>. Or click the hyperlink name of a region, such as the <u>Middle East</u>, and then continue clicking to select your choices as more specific geographic areas appear on-screen — for example, click <u>Weather</u> ☞ <u>Asia</u> ☞ <u>Thailand</u> ☞ <u>Bangkok</u>.

Figure 6-2:   By visiting Yahoo! Weather, you can check the weather conditions anywhere in the world.

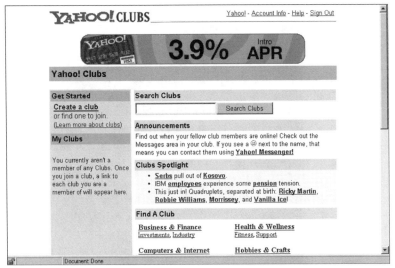

After you reach your city of interest, you see a listing of the current conditions at the location, such as temperature, wind speed, and humidity, along with a four-day forecast. You also see a series of Maps and Images such as Satellite, Precipitation, and Pollen maps. Clicking any of these thumbnail maps opens a larger image providing the details for that map.

Mapping out directions

Regardless of what neighborhood you live in (or visit), local townies are always willing to provide you with driving directions for "the best way" to get somewhere. So that you don't need to stop, roll down the window, and endure conflicting commentary, Yahoo! provides you maps for navigating almost anywhere you want to go. Access Yahoo! Maps by using either of the following methods:

■ At the Yahoo! home page (at `www.yahoo.com`), click the <u>Maps</u> hyperlink in the Frequently Accessed Categories area at the top of the page.

■ Type `http://maps.yahoo.com` in your browser and press Enter or Return.

At the Yahoo! Maps page, you see the following two options for displaying maps to help you find your way:

■ **Map a new Address:** In the blank boxes, type the street address or intersection and the city/state/zip or just the zip of the location for which you want a map. Alternatively, you may enter an airport code, such as LAX or DCA (see Figure 6-3), to obtain a map for the area surrounding that airport. Click the Get Map button to show a map of your chosen area. Click the left-facing arrows to zoom out on the map or click the right-facing arrows to zoom in. Click the <u>Printable Map</u> hyperlink to open a printable version of your selected map.

■ **Driving Directions:** Click the <u>Driving Directions</u> hyperlink on the main Maps page to access the Driving Directions page. In the blank boxes, type the starting address and the destination address. For each address, include the street address or intersection and the city/state/zip or just the zip code of the location for which you want a map.

Figure 6-3: The Maps Area enables you to print out maps and driving directions.

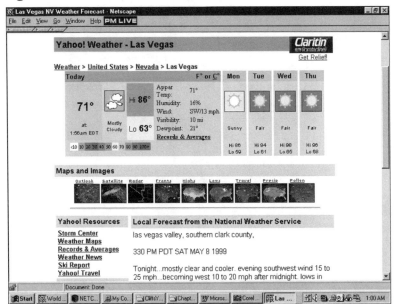

Checking Out Yahooligans!

The Web is a place for everyone, including kids, so Yahoo!
contains a special areas within its Web site just for young people. This special area, *Yahooligans!*, is a combination children's
library, exploration haven, playground, and personal tutor.

Go to Yahooligans! (shown in Figure 6-4) by using either of
the following procedures:

■ At the Yahoo! home page (at www.yahoo.com), click
the <u>Yahooligans!</u> hyperlink in the Others Guides area at
the bottom of the page.

■ Type www.yahooligans.com in your browser and
press Enter or Return.

Figure 6-4: Yahooligans! is the Yahoo! site for kids.

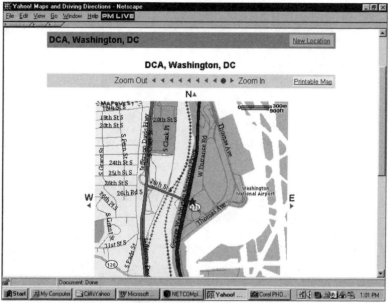

Yahooligans! is free of pornographic and vulgar material, and parents can feel a relative sense of security about their little ones browsing amok in its vast, kid-friendly categories.

Parents should still keep in mind that any Yahoo! user can attend the Net Events listed in Yahooligans! For this reason, you may want to monitor your children's participation in Net Events to keep tabs on whom they're chatting with and what information is being exchanged.

CHAPTER 7
ATTENDING YAHOO! NET EVENTS

IN THIS CHAPTER

- Accessing the Net Events directory
- Checking out what's on
- Tuning in a live broadcast
- Chatting in a chat room
- Suggesting a Net Event
- Scheduling Net Events in Yahoo! Calendar

Everyone loves a special event, and Yahoo! users are no different. With Yahoo! Net Events, you can listen to live concerts, engage in a little "coffee talk," watch a televised interview, and attend hundreds of other Web events in real-time. Now, instead of going out, you can go online to take part in entertaining, educational, and informational live activities. And instead of traveling to a big city — or missing out because you can't physically travel — you and other Yahoo!s congregate together in cyberspace as an audience of desktop participants. Knowing what events are on — and when they're on — is made easy with the Yahoo! directory of Net Events.

The Net Events directory provides you with comprehensive schedules that tell you everything you need to know about upcoming Net Events: dates, times, where to "tune in," event synopses, and associated Web sites. With the Net Events directory, you can locate events in the subject indexes, or you can search for specific events using keywords. Sometimes, you can even access events that have already taken place —

if the event sponsors choose to make archives available. The directory also tells you what resources you need to participate in particular events. For instance, you may need a special plug-in or software program to listen to a live radio broadcast.

Accessing the Net Events Directory

The Yahoo! directory of Net Events is available on the Net Events page. Use either of the following methods to summon the Yahoo! Net Events page, as shown in Figure 7-1:

- At the Yahoo! home page (www.yahoo.com), choose Net Events from the Other Guides area at the bottom of the page.

- Type http://events.yahoo.com in your browser and press Enter or Return.

Figure 7-1: The Net Events page is where you find out what's on in Yahoo!.

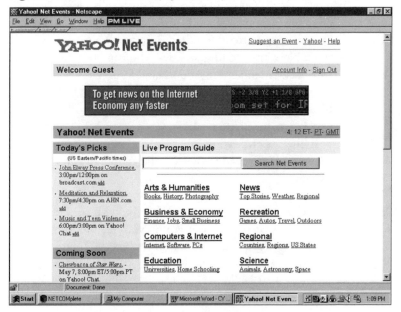

If you haven't signed in to Yahoo! with your ID and password, the Net Events page greets you with `Welcome Guest`. Otherwise, it greets you using your Yahoo! ID.

Many of the functions you perform relating to Net Events — such as adding events to your Yahoo! Calendar — require you to sign in. (See Chapter 1 for additional information on signing in.)

In the Yahoo! Net Events banner, the current time appears. If you plan to participate in scheduled events, you need to know what time it is! You can display this time in ET (Eastern Time), PT (Pacific Time), or GMT (Greenwich Mean Time). Just click ET, PT, or GMT to display the current time accordingly.

Checking Out What's On

Net Events offers a veritable smorgasbord of concerts, broadcasts, games, chats, and other activities you can attend. Figure 7-2 gives you an idea of how broad is the range of topics.

Figure 7-2:   Check out upcoming Net Events in the Recreation category.

Programs on Sun, May 2					9: 38 ET-PT- GMT	
←	Sat 1	Sun 2	Mon 3	Tue 4	Wed 5	Thu 6	→

6:00am Building the Log Cabin ⟵⟳ - watch the construction of a log home. Daily journal of events showing each step of the log home construction. Java Cam. *The Log Cam*.add

10:00am The Travel Show ⟵⟳ - learn the tips and tricks needed to travel the world in comfort. RealPlayer. *broadcast.com*.add

5:00pm Auto World ⟵⟳ - Bob Long examines America's love of the automobile in this entertaining and informative program. RealPlayer. *broadcast.com*.add

Chat Rooms	Open 24 hours

• Lotto Chat - chat about your favorite numbers. Java Chat. *lottery.com*.

more...

The Net Events are categorized into the following areas on the main Net Events page:

■ **Today's Picks:** This short list shows what Net Events are taking place on the current date. The title of each event is hyperlinked to a Web page supplying additional information or directly to the event itself. Clicking the <u>Add</u> hyperlink for any event opens Yahoo! Calendar and adds the event to your Calendar.

■ **Coming Soon:** This list shows upcoming Net Events that will take place in the near future (usually, within the next week). The title of the event is hyperlinked to a Web page supplying additional information on the event. Click the <u>suggest an event...</u> hyperlink to post a new Net Event for listing. Clicking this hyperlink summons the Add to Yahoo! Net Events page where you must complete a form and click Submit to suggest your event.

■ **Inside Yahoo!:** This page provides hyperlinks to cool events — net and otherwise — happening now. It also provides a hyperlink to Yahoo! Calendar so that you can jot down and keep track of your busy schedule of events. See Table 7-1 for more information about what's in this area.

■ **Live Program Guide:** Provides Yahoo! users with a familiar directory of 14 categories (**Arts & Humanities**, **Business & Economy**, and so on) that serves as the framework for organizing Net Events by subject area. (See Chapter 2 for more information on the Yahoo! directory.) You can click any category to find listings for Net Events featuring the subject matter of the category. Alternatively, you can type a keyword and click the Search Net Events button to locate specific events.

Table 7-1:   Hyperlinks on the Inside Yahoo! Page

Click This	*To Do This*
Y! Calendar	Open the Calendar page where you can record the date and time of important events. You can even have Calendar send you reminders of events as they approach (see Chapter 10 for details).
Y! Chat	Opens the Chat page where you can participate in live chat sessions with fellow Yahoo! users. The Yahoo! Chat page provides a short list of Net Events in the Upcoming Events area. Click the Events Calendar hyperlink to obtain details and hyperlinks for these events.
Y! Full Coverage	Open the Yahoo! News Full Coverage page, which presents links to the latest news stories that people are talking about. Clicking a story opens the associated Web page, and many stories have hyperlinks to the Message Board where you can read and post messages relating to the story.
Y! Internet Live	Go to today's live — and very hip — events from Yahoo! Internet Life. This area typically appeals to Yahoo! users who consider themselves part of the eclectic set.
Y! Local Events	Offers events on real things happening in your hometown. You can click the major metro area where you live or search for specific events.
Y! Movie Showtimes	Find out what's playing on the big screen at a theater near you. You supply your area code, and Yahoo! supplies the showtimes, synopses, and reviews for movies playing in your vicinity.
Y! TV Coverage	Check listings for television programming airing on your local stations.

Tuning In to a Live Broadcast

Participating in a live broadcast may or may not require additional software beyond your Web browser. If a Net Event that you want to attend requires you to download plug-ins or extra programs, the information page for the event tells you what you need — and typically provides hyperlinks to the download sites. After you download and install specialized software, you have it available for any future Net Events that require the same software. In other words, you don't have to download something every time you participate in an event.

No additional software required

Some live broadcasts don't require that you download any special software at all. Net Events such as Chats or activity chronicles that display constantly updated photos (such as the construction of a log cabin) need no additional software for you to participate in them.

Additional software required

For some Net Events, you need special software. RealPlayer is probably the most frequently used software application for Net Events, because it allows you to tap into *streaming video and audio*. When a Net Event is broadcast in RealPlayer, you can view and hear the event as it happens — kind of like watching live television.

Net Events that require RealPlayer generally have a button that you can click to download the necessary software, such as the button shown in Figure 7-3. Follow the installation instructions in the program to install it. The RealPlayer Web site, www.realplayer.com, provides additional information on using RealPlayer software.

Figure 7-3:   Events that require special software contain links to the software.

You can find audio and video broadcast Net Events by click-ing the <u>Audio/Video Channels</u> hyperlink in the Live Program Guide area of the main Net Events page.

Chatting in a Chat Room

Yahoo! Chat is an online gathering place where you and other Yahoo! users can chew the fat over everything from current events to favorite pastimes. The online location where folks get together to chat is called a *chat room*. And like a house with many different rooms, Yahoo! has many different chat rooms, each dedicated to a specific topic.

Some chat rooms are open 24 hours a day, 7 days a week. Many chats, though, transpire as structured discussions, with each discussion scheduled for a specific date and time.

Looking around Yahoo! Chat

You can access Yahoo! Chat by clicking on any chat event listed on the Net Page, or you can go directly to the Chat page using any of these methods:

■   At the Yahoo! home page (www.yahoo.com), click the <u>Chat</u> hyperlink in the Frequently Accessed Categories area at the top of the page.

■   At the Yahoo! Net Events page (http://events. yahoo.com), click the <u>Y! Chat</u> hyperlink in the Inside Yahoo! area.

■ Type http://chat.yahoo.com in your browser and press Enter or Return.

The first time you use Yahoo! Chat, you're asked to read and agree to Yahoo!'s rules for using the chat rooms. This agreement basically states that you won't harass anyone in the chat rooms, impersonate other Yahoo! users, disrupt the chat session, or send illegal documents online.

Participating in Chat requires that you sign in. If you haven't signed in to Yahoo! prior to entering Chat, you need to type in your ID and Password before participating in a chat session.

Two main areas of the Welcome to Yahoo! Chat page (see Figure 7-4) are Featured Rooms and Upcoming Events.

Figure 7-4:   Getting started with Yahoo! Chat.

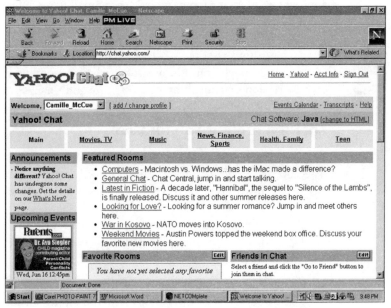

Here's what each area offers:

■ **Featured Rooms:** Provides a list of the most popular chat rooms.

If none of the featured rooms interest you, scroll down the Chat page and click the <u>complete room list</u> hyperlink for a more comprehensive listing of available chat rooms.) Just click your choice to enter the chat room and begin chatting.

■ **Upcoming Events:** Provides short descriptions of chat events scheduled to take place in the near future. To find out more about these events, check out the chat Events Calendar. You can summon this calendar by clicking the <u>Events Calendar</u> hyperlink at the top of the Yahoo! Chat page. (See "Scheduling Net Events in Yahoo! Calendar" later in this chapter to learn how to enter these events into your personal Calendar.)

If you choose to chat using Java as your Chat Software (the preferred option), be patient while the Java applet loads. You may have to wait a few seconds before you can enter the chat room.

Chatting away

Upon entering a chat room, you see an interface like the one shown in Figure 7-5, and your name appears in the Chatters list. You also see a running dialogue of the chat, with the name of each chatter followed by his or her comment. The running dialogue also keeps tabs on chatters as they enter or exit the chat room.

Figure 7-5: A chat in progress.

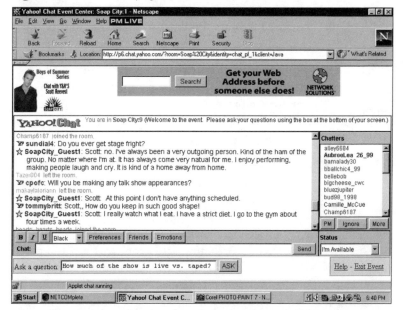

Table 7-2 shows you some of the actions you can take in the chat room.

Table 7-2: Understanding the Chat Interface

To Do This	Do This
Read the running dialog	Drag the slider bar up and down to review comments
Send a message	Type your message in the empty chat box just below the chat window, and click the Send button
Format your messages	Click the Bold, Italic, or Underline button just above the chat box to format the text of your messages. Click the arrow next to the word *Black* to display a text color drop-down menu.

To Do This	Do This
Express an emotion	Click the Emotions button just above the chat box to display an Emotions window that provides a long list of emotions. Select an emotion and click the Emote User button to express your chosen emotion.
Read the profile of a chatter	Select the name of the chatter in the chat window (*not* the Chatters list) to summon the Select Action window; then click the View Profile button.
Send a private message	Select the name of the chatter in the chat window to summon the Select Action window; then click the Private Message button. Type your message in the blank area and press the Send button. Private messages are not viewable by other chatters, only the individual you are contacting privately.
Ignore/stop ignoring a chatter	Click the name of the chatter in the chat window to summon the Select Action window; then select or deselect the Ignore check box. Ignoring a chatter allows you to filter out comments from someone you find annoying or harassing.
Exit the chat room	Click the Exit hyperlink at the bottom of the screen, or click the Back button in your browser to return to the main Yahoo! Chat page.

Tip

You can navigate quickly to the Yahoo! directory of chat rooms by clicking the Chat Rooms hyperlink in the Live Program Guide area of the main Net Events page.

Scheduling Net Events in Yahoo! Calendar

Many Net Events offer an <u>add</u> hyperlink or an <u>Add to my Calendar</u> hyperlink listed beside the event name. Clicking such a hyperlink adds the event to your personal Yahoo! Calendar. (If you haven't yet signed in to Calendar, you're asked to do so before the event is added.) You can then view the event on your Calendar and set up Calendar to send you a reminder via e-mail or pager as the event approaches. See Chapter 10 for more information about the Yahoo! calendar.

CHAPTER 8
USING YAHOO! MESSENGER

IN THIS CHAPTER

- Obtaining and installing the Messenger software
- Finding friends to page
- Keeping abreast of e-mail, news, and stock prices
- Sending and receiving instant messages

Think of Yahoo! Messenger as a way to "talk" — via instantaneous e-mail — to any other Yahoo! with an Instant Messenger in the world . . . for free! You conduct Yahoo! Messenger conversations by typing and not by speaking, and your Yahoo! friends can see what you type just as you type it. You can add anyone with a Yahoo! Messenger to your *Friends list*, which enables you to page them and vice-versa. You can even set up conference "calls," in which multiple Yahoos! chat simultaneously.

Yahoo! Messenger also functions like a "regular" Messenger for your desktop in that you can page friends to see who's currently online and available for chatting. You can even set up Messenger to inform you the moment that you receive Yahoo! Mail or a Calendar reminder. And for those who require the most up-to-the-minute information, you can customize Messenger to alert you to the latest Stock quotes, News updates, and sports Scoreboard tallies.

Getting Started with Yahoo! Messenger

The Yahoo! Messenger is really cool and easy to use, but getting it up and running may be the most difficult part of using it. First, you need certain things to make it run.

If you're a Windows user, you need the following items:

■ The Yahoo! Messenger program, which is available for download and installation from Yahoo!. See the next section for more information on downloading the Yahoo! Messenger program.

■ Netscape Navigator (3.0 or later) or Microsoft Internet Explorer (3.0 or later).

If you're a Mac or UNIX user, you need the following:

■ Netscape Navigator (3.0 or later) or Microsoft Internet Explorer (3.01 or later).

■ Both Java and Javascript enabled in your browser.

Mac and Unix users (and Windows users, if they want to run the Java version of the Messenger) don't need to download or install anything. Just click the <u>Use the Macintosh, Unix, Java Edition</u> hyperlink in the Frequently Accessed Categories area on the Yahoo! home page. The Windows version loads more quickly than the Java version.

The Java version of the Messenger looks slightly different from the Windows version.

Downloading and installing the Yahoo! Messenger

If you want to use the standard Windows version of the Messenger, you need to download the YMSGRIE.EXE program from Yahoo!. Follow these steps to download the Messenger:

1. Click the <u>Messenger</u> hyperlink in the Frequently
Accessed Categories area on the Yahoo! home page. The
Yahoo! Messenger page appears, as shown in Figure 8-1.

Figure 8-1:   The Yahoo! Messenger page.

2. Click the <u>Instructions for Windows 95/NT/98 Users</u>
hyperlink to begin the download. The Viewing Location
dialog box appears and stays with you through the download.

3. After the download finishes, a Save As dialog box appears,
in which you can choose a location for saving the Messenger program. The file name is YMSGRIE.EXE.

4. Click Save to save the file at your designated location.

After you have the file safely on your hard drive, you can
install the program. To do so, just follow these steps:

1. Double-click the YMSGRIE.EXE program icon to start the Messenger program installation.

2. Click the Next button in the Messenger Welcome screen, which takes you to the Terms of Service screen.

3. Click the I Accept button to proceed to the Select Destination Directory screen, where you choose a location for the program.

4. Click Next to accept the default location for the program; or choose your own location for the program by clicking the Browse button, double-clicking folders to choose a location for the program, and then clicking the Next button.

5. In the Ready to Install! screen, you can decide how you want the Yahoo! Messenger to function by selecting either or both of the following check boxes (or leaving them blank) and then clicking the Next button.

    Leaving the Do Not Run Automatically When I Start My Computer check box blank causes Messenger to run automatically each time you boot your computer. Leaving the Do Not Attempt or Accept Direct Connections with My Friends on Messenger check blank box enables Messenger to automatically connect you with persons on your Friends list.

Your choices for starting Messenger aren't set in stone — you can change them at any time from the Messenger menu bar by choosing Preferences⇨Edit.

The Yahoo! Messenger installation swings into action. The installation places a shortcut to the Messenger on your desktop. For easy access, Yahoo! Messenger also now appears in your Windows Start menu.

Starting the Messenger

The first time you install the Messenger, it starts automatically and takes you to the Login screen. After that, depending on how you configure the Messenger, it may start automatically after you start your computer. (If it doesn't now and you decide that you do want the Messenger to start automatically, choose Preferences⊅Edit).

If the Messenger doesn't start automatically, you can use one of the following methods to start the Yahoo! Messenger:

- ◼ Double-click the Messenger shortcut on the Windows desktop.

- ◼ Choose Start⊅Yahoo! Messenger from the Windows Start menu.

Starting the Messenger opens the Yahoo! Messenger dialog box. Just click OK to close this dialog box and proceed with logging in and using the Messenger.

If you tire of seeing the Yahoo! Messenger dialog box, click the Show This Dialog Box in the Future check box to deselect it. The dialog box no longer appears after you start the Messenger.

Logging into the Messenger

After you start the Yahoo! Messenger, you must enter your login information into the Login dialog box, as shown in Figure 8-2.

Figure 8-2: The Login dialog box.

You must complete the information in this dialog box to begin using the Messenger. Here are your options:

■ **New User?** Click the Get a Yahoo! ID button if you don't have a Yahoo! ID yet. A Sign Up! page appears and leads you through the process of getting your very own Yahoo! ID. (See Chapter 1 for additional information.)

■ **Already have a Yahoo! ID?** If you have a Yahoo ID, type the ID and Password in the appropriate text boxes of the Login dialog box and then click the Login button.

If you already have a Yahoo! ID, you can select the Remember My ID & Password check box in the Login dialog box to bypass the login step in the future.

The Yahoo! Messenger consists of the following three areas:

■ **Menu bar:** Menu options are uniquely tailored for each Messenger tab but always include Login, Edit, Y!, and Help.

■ **Information window:** This window lists the Messenger information that's unique to each tab, such as Friends Online on the Friends tab or Stock Quotes on the Stocks tab.

- **Messenger tabs:** Tabs consist of Friends, Stocks, News, Scoreboard, and Overview. As do tabs in a three-ring binder, Messenger tabs enable you to quickly locate and access each information area of the Messenger.

- **Connection status:** This area indicates whether your Messenger is connected and available for use or disconnected. You use the Login item on the Messenger menu bar to connect and disconnect your Messenger.

Increasing Your Circle of Friends

If you know a friend's Yahoo! ID or e-mail address, you can invite him (or her!) to get a Yahoo! Messenger. You can add any friends who also possess a Messenger to your Friends list so that you can engage in online chat. To invite a friend to get Yahoo! Messenger, follow these steps:

1. In Messenger, click the Friends tab.

2. From the Messenger menu bar, choose Messenger➪Invite a Friend to Sign Up or press Ctrl+I. This command opens the Invite a Friend to Use Yahoo! Messenger page.

3. Type your friend's e-mail address, Yahoo! or otherwise.

4. Select your Yahoo! ID from the drop-down list so that your friend knows who's sending the invitation. (All your different Yahoo! IDs appear in the drop-down list.)

5. Type your real name if you want your friend to know who you really are. (He may not know from your Yahoo! ID alone.)

6. Type a message to send with the invitation.

7. Click the Invite Friend button to send the invitation to your friend.

Listing pals on your Friends list

After a friend has Yahoo! Messenger, you can add that friend to your Friends list by using the following steps:

1. In Messenger, click the Friends tab.

2. Click the Add button. This action opens the Add a Friend/Group dialog box.

3. Type your friend's Yahoo! ID into the Your Friend's Yahoo! ID box. You have to supply a Yahoo! ID here rather than another e-mail address.

4. Add your friend to a group by clicking the arrow next to the Group box and selecting a group from the drop-down list. To create a new group (for example, colleagues, sorority sisters, fly-fishing friends, and so on), type the name of the new group in the text box.

5. Type the name for yourself that you want your friend to see in his Friends list in the Select Your Yahoo! ID box. If you have several Yahoo! IDs, you need to pick one.

6. Type a message into the Message box that tells your friend that you're adding him to your Messenger's Friends list. (Your friend should consider this good news . . . unless, of course, you're some sort of online stalker.)

7. Click the Add button and the dialog box closes.

Your friend is now on your Messenger's Friends list.

Searching for new friends

You can locate individuals to add to your Messenger's Friends list by searching the Public Profiles of other Yahoo! users. A Public Profile provides basic information about a Yahoo! user such as his or her name, Yahoo! ID, and personal interests. To conduct a Basic Search, follow these steps:

1. Open the Messenger and click the Friends tab to open the Search Public Profiles page.

2. Type information into only one of the three available text boxes: Yahoo! ID, Name, or Keywords. Typing something like **Beagles** or **diving** in the Keywords text box locates users who indicate interests in specific hobbies, sports, and so on.

3. Click the down arrow to the right of the text box in which you type this information and select the group to search — either All Users or just Messenger Users.

4. Click the Search button to execute your search.

Yahoo! returns results for all persons matching your designated criteria. You can then start a dialogue with these individuals via Mail or Messenger to determine whether you want to add them to your Friends list.

You can conduct a more extensive search — adding limiting criteria such as location and age — by clicking the Power Search button on the Search Public Profiles page.

Set up your own Public Profile so that other Yahoo! users know who you are! Just click the Friends tab in Messenger and then click the Profiles button and select Edit my profiles.

Changing your status

As does the In/Out board that you see in many office places, Messenger provides you with a way of informing Yahoo! Friends of your availability for online chats. Your options include everything from **I'm Available** to **Out to Lunch**. To set your availability, click the Friends tab and then click the Availability Status button and choose a status from the list. The Status Change Confirmation dialog box appears to confirm your change. Click OK. You can change your availability as often as you want.

Sending and Receiving Instant Messages

Instant messages make it easy to contact your friends in real time via your computer for a quick text chat. You have to add your friend to your Friends list before you can send the instant message. The previous section explains how to add friends to your list.

Sending instant messages

To send an instant message to a friend, follow these steps:

1. At the Friends tab, double-click the Yahoo ID of the person on your Friends list to whom you want to send a message. A Send Instant Message window opens. The To text box displays your friend's Yahoo! ID and the From text box displays your Yahoo! ID.

2. Click the Change Text Color button (which looks like a painter's palette) or the Bold, Italic, or Underline buttons to format the message text that you're going to type.

3. Type your message in the window and click Send. Yahoo! instantly delivers your message to your friend.

If your friend is offline at the time that you send your instant message, Yahoo! stores the message and delivers it the next time your friend opens Messenger.

You can engage multiple friends in the exchange of instant messages by clicking the Chat Room button on the Instant Message window. This action opens the Start a Chat Room window, where you can add friends and invite them to a join a chat.

Receiving and replying to instant messages

Whenever you're using Yahoo! Messenger and a friend sends you an instant message, an Instant Message dialog box appears, showing the name of the sender and the text of the message. If you're offline at the time your friend sends an instant message, Yahoo! stores the message and delivers it the next time that you open your Messenger. You can view previous messages at any time by clicking the Message button (on the Friends tab) and selecting View Stored Messages.

Reply to an instant message as shown in Figure 8-3 by clicking the Reply button in the Instant Message window, typing your response, and clicking Send.

Figure 8-3:   Replying to an instant message.

You can change the appearance of your response text by clicking the Change Text Color button (which looks like a painter's palette) or the Bold, Italics, or Underline buttons to format the text that you type. These formatting buttons always lie just above the area of any window in which you type your instant message.

Yahoo! Messenger has added a new feature that allows you to conduct voice chats. To access this feature, go to the Messenger menu bar and select Messenger➪Start a Voice Chat.

Receiving Alerts

You can configure Yahoo! Messenger to provide you with constantly updated stock prices, news headlines, and sports scores. To view information for each of these items, you must enable the News, Stocks, and Scoreboard tabs in your Messenger by following these steps:

1. Choose Edit⊏⟩Preferences to open the Preferences dialog box and then click the Appearance tab.

2. In the Show These Tabs in Messenger area, click the check box next to each tab that you want to include. (You can choose among Stocks, News, and Scoreboard.)

3. Click OK to establish your update choices and close the Preferences dialog box.

Remember

Your Messenger updates reflect the current selections for Stocks, News, and Sports for My Yahoo!. You can edit stock choices by clicking the Stocks tab in Messenger and choosing Stocks⊏⟩Edit My Portfolios from the Messenger menu bar. You can edit news choices by clicking the News tab and choosing News⊏⟩Edit News Settings from the Messenger menu bar. You can edit Sports choices by clicking the Scoreboard tab and choosing Sports⊏⟩Edit Sports Settings from the Messenger menu bar. Tab-specific menus appear for the currently-selected tab in Messenger.

Obtaining mail alerts

You can configure Yahoo! Messenger to alert you whenever a new mail message arrives in Mail. Just follow these steps:

1. Open the Preferences dialog box by choosing Edit⊏⟩Preferences from the Messenger menu bar and then click the Mail tab.

2. Select a radio button in the Alert Me area. You can have the Messenger check every so many minutes (you choose a number) or alert you every time you receive a new message.

3. Select how you want Messenger to deliver your alert by clicking the check box of your choice. Messenger can display an icon on the right side of the Windows taskbar, display a dialog box, or play a sound. If you really want to make certain that you don't miss new mail, you can check all three!

4. Click OK to establish your mail-alert choices and close the Preferences dialog box.

Receiving news updates

The News tab of Yahoo! Messenger lists the latest news headlines to keep you up-to-date on what's happening around the world. The headlines originate from the news sources you set up in My Yahoo! In fact, the Messenger News tab is basically a mirror of the My Front Page Headlines area in My Yahoo! (See Chapter 4 for more information on choosing your news sources.) You can view any news story listed in the Messenger by clicking its headline's hyperlink. The story will open in your browser.

Receiving stock alerts

You can set up Yahoo! Messenger to send you an alert whenever the price or volume of one of your selected stocks varies within parameters that you set. To receive stock alerts, follow these steps:

1. Open the Preferences dialog box by choosing Edit➪Preferences from the Messenger menu bar.

2. In the Preferences dialog box, click the Stocks tab.

3. If it's not already selected, click in the Show Tab and Enable Alerts for Stocks check box to select it.

4. Click any of the check boxes to indicate when you want Messenger to deliver your alert. Your choices are My Stocks Trip an Upper or Lower Limit, Volume for Any Stock Is (*a percentage that you designate*) over Average Daily Volume, and Price change for the Day is Greater Than (*a percentage that you designate*).

5. Select check boxes to indicate how you want Messenger to deliver your alert. Choices are Display a Taskbar "Tray" Icon, Display a Dialog Box, and Play a Sound.

6. Click OK to establish your stock alerts and close the Preferences dialog box.

YAHOO! SERVICES

Like a gigantic mall of the Internet, Yahoo! offers an enormous collection of commercial shops and services where you can perform almost any business transaction you can dream up. With Yahoo! Services you can peruse and purchase merchandise in online stores. You can attend online auctions, post and read classified ads, and even buy and sell real estate and automobiles. And for the entrepreneurs among you, Yahoo! has a special area for small businesses that's chock full of advice, communications tools, and promotional resources.

Yahoo! Services also offers you everything you need to assemble and track a financial portfolio, and find new employment — perhaps if the portfolio is performing poorly! And if the portfolio is doing well . . . then you can use Yahoo!'s Travel Agent services to book a trip for an indulging getaway!

Shopping online

Why brave bad traffic, lousy parking, and annoying shoppers when you can shop online? Yahoo! Shopping lets you stroll through thousands of the world's greatest stores, page by page, checking out the latest products without ever stepping foot outside your humble abode. Even better, Shopping lets you purchase selected items online with your credit card for delivery direct to you — no lugging packages through the parking lot! Access Yahoo! Shopping using one of the following methods:

- At the Yahoo! home page (www.yahoo.com), click the <u>Shopping</u> hyperlink in the Frequently Accessed Categories area at the top of the page.

- Type http://shopping.yahoo.com into your browser and press Enter or Return.

Locating items to purchase

The Yahoo! Shopping page presents several areas where you can begin your buying bonanza. Hot purchase items are listed at the top of the page, followed by a list of New Featured Stores and Shopping Categories. The Shopping Categories area consists of 14 top-level categories, plus a search box. Each top-level shopping category is composed of several lower-level categories.

To search for a specific item within the shopping categories, first type the name of the item in the Categories search box and select a search category from the drop-down list. Then click the Search button to obtain a list of matches for your request. You can click any hyperlink in the list of matches to view more information on that item.

Selecting and buying items

When you locate an item you wish to purchase, follow these steps to record and send in your order:

1. At the description page for the item you want to buy, click the Order button. Yahoo! adds the item to your shopping cart, as shown in Figure 9-1. The shopping cart keeps a list of each item you select for purchase, the store that sells the item, options (such as size, color), the unit price, the quantity you are purchasing, and the item subtotal. To change the quantity of an item, type the number you want into the Quantity box and click the Update Quantities button. The subtotal for that item also updates.

Figure 9-1:   Items you select for purchase are added to your shopping cart.

2. Click the Keep Shopping button to return to the online stores and continue shopping, clicking the Order button and adding items to your shopping cart until you finish.

3. To take items out of your shopping cart, click the Remove button next to each item you want to discard.

4. When you finish adding items to your shopping cart, click the Place Order button. If you haven't yet signed in, Yahoo! prompts to do so before continuing. If instead you want to place your order without signing in, click the Place Order Without Registering button. At the Yahoo! Shopping Check Out page, review your order and provide a payment method and shipping information for each company from which you order.

5. Click the Send This Order button to confirm and send your order, or click the Do Not Order button to cancel the order.

Remember

You have to complete a separate form for each company with which you want to place an order. Doing so enables you to choose different delivery addresses and different payment methods for each company.

Attending online auctions

Although participating in online auctions is not as much fun as hearing live auctioneers work their tongue-twisting magic, Yahoo! Auctions provides you with an online way to bid on, buy, and sell unique and rare items. You have to bid against a cadre of other Yahoo!s vying for the same merchandise, but if you're successful, you may finally acquire that "antique" free-standing Ms. Pac Man game you've had your eye on!

Access Yahoo! Auctions using one of the following methods:

■ At the Yahoo! home page (www.yahoo.com), choose Auctions from the Hot Topics at the top of the page.

■ Type http://auctions.yahoo.com into your browser and press Enter or Return.

The Yahoo! Auctions main page consists of the following areas:

- **Auction Services:** This area provides a hyperlink for My Auctions, which gives you a summary of items you're currently bidding on, auctions you have recently won, and auctions that have recently closed. It also provides hyperlinks for Bidder's Guide and Seller's Guide, which explain the rules for bidding on items and placing items up for bid.

- **Featured Auction:** This area provides a hyperlink to the auction area of a very desirable, in-demand item.

- **Charity Auction:** This area provides hyperlinks to several auctions that raise funds for worthy causes.

- **Search Auctions:** In this area, you type an item you want to find that's being auctioned off and click Search. Auctions for exact matches and related items are listed.

- **Browse Auctions:** This area is divided into browseable categories — much like the rest of Yahoo! You can click through categories to find auctions that interest you. Each category title is accompanied by a number in parentheses that tells the number of auctions taking place for that particular category. You can also click the Full Category Index hyperlink for a complete listing of all available Auction categories. For example, Figure 9-2 shows just how esoteric auction categories can get!

Figure 9-2: Bid on, buy, and sell items in an online auction.

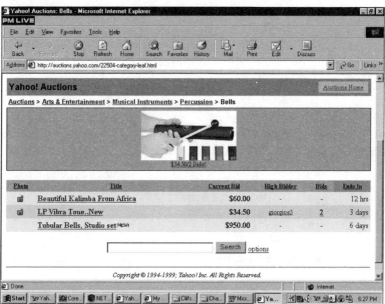

Reading the Classifieds

Yahoo! Classifieds are a nationwide version of the classified ads you find in your Sunday paper. If you have an item you want to sell, a lost dog you want to find, or a high school reunion you want to announce (as in Figure 9-3), Yahoo! Classifieds is the place for you.

Figure 9-3: Post your announcement in the Yahoo! Classifieds.

DATE	TYPE	AD TITLE	LOCATION	FULL LISTING
05/17/99	Reunions	Brighton High School "Class of 1980"	Boston, Massachusetts	More detail
05/12/99	Reunions	Hopatcong NJ HS Class of 1974 Reunion	Boston, Massachusetts	More detail
05/09/99	Reunions	ARC NAFAS Aquatic School Grads	Wellesley, Massachusetts	More detail

◄ Previous Ads | Next Ads ►

Access Yahoo! Classifieds using one of the following methods:

- At the Yahoo! home page (www.yahoo.com), click the Classifieds hyperlink in the Frequently Accessed Categories area at the top of the page.

■ Type `http://classifieds.yahoo.com` into your browser and press Enter or Return.

Perusing the ads

You can view the Yahoo! Classifieds page either by Region or by Category (just like in a newspaper). To select how you want to view the Classifieds, click the View by hyperlink in the Listings area. Here's what each View by option offers:

■ **View by Region:** Clicking this option summons a listing of major U.S. metropolitan areas. You can click any area to obtain classified listings by persons living in the vicinity of the selected metro area.

■ **View by Category:** Clicking this option summons a listing of 14 general classified categories. Listings in each category are posted by individuals living virtually anywhere. Depending on the category, a search option may be available, which enables you to limit the category listings to geographic regions you define.

Ads that match the subject matter you seek can appear in a summary table or as detailed listings. Click the Tabled Results hyperlink or the Detailed Results hyperlink at the top of the Search Results page to choose how you want your classifieds presented. Click any listing to obtain additional details about the listing, including a contact person, reply e-mail, and sometimes a related photograph.

Responding to an ad

If you want to obtain more information on a listing or to contact the person who listed the ad, you can respond to the ad. Instead of calling the person as you may do for a "regular" classified listing, you simply click the Reply to this ad hyperlink located at the end of a listing. An e-mail template appears with the From (that's you!) and To (the ad's lister) e-mail addresses already filled in. Type your response to the ad in the blank Your Reply Here area. When you finish, click the Send Message button to deliver your message, or click Cancel to discard the message.

Posting your own ad

If you have an item you want to sell, an announcement you want to make, or other listing appropriate to the Yahoo! Classifieds, you can post your own ad online. Just follow these steps:

1. At the Classifieds main page, click the <u>Submit Ads</u> hyperlink.

2. At the Submission page, click a category in which you want your ad to be listed. The categories are identical to those on the Classifieds main page with one exception: An additional category exists for <u>Employment Wanted</u>.

3. Supply the requested information to Yahoo! regarding details of your listing. Some categories (such as Air & Water Craft) require that you select a more specific, lower-level category for your listing. Others (such as Employment Wanted) require that you provide your zip code so that you can be categorized by geographic region. All categories ask you to provide contact information so that individuals interested in pursuing your listing can reply to your ad.

4. Click the Submit entry button to complete the listing of your ad. Your ad is listed free of charge in the Yahoo! Classifieds.

You can edit an ad you have listed at any time by clicking the <u>Edit Ads</u> hyperlink in Yahoo! Classifieds.

Buying and Selling an Automobile

Yahoo! Autos is your one-stop shopping guide for cars, SUVs, and trucks. In fact, Figure 9-4 shows you that Autos is sort of a combination *Consumer Reports,* glossy brochure, *Blue Book,* certified mechanic, and loan officer. Whether you're in the market as a buyer or seller, Yahoo! Autos provides you with everything you need to know about automobiles — both new and used.

Figure 9-4:   Check out Yahoo! Autos for all your auto selling and buying needs.

Access Yahoo! Autos using one of the following methods:

- At the Yahoo! home page (www.yahoo.com), click the Autos hyperlink in the Other Guides area at the bottom of the page.

- Type http://autos.yahoo.com into your browser and press Enter or Return.

Buying and Selling Real Estate

The home market has taken a new direction with the explosion of the Web. Now, instead of relying on homebuilders or real estate agents for leads, you can take charge of both buying and selling a home with resources available through Yahoo! Real Estate.

Access Yahoo! Real Estate using one of the following methods:

- At the Yahoo! home page (`www.yahoo.com`), click the Real Estate hyperlink from Other Guides at the bottom of the page.

- Type `http://realestate.yahoo.com` into your browser and press Enter or Return.

Real Estate provides several valuable informational areas you may want to explore, including the following:

- **Resources:** This area includes hyperlinks to City Maps and City Profiles of areas you may want to move to. It also includes a Glossary hyperlink to assist you in deciphering the real estate lingo.

- **Features:** This area includes hyperlinks listing Houses for Sales and Apartments for Rent. It also provides a City Comparison hyperlink where you can select and compare a variety of data for two U.S. cities, including population, cost of living, crime rate, average home cost, and taxes. Additionally, the School Reports hyperlink provides data such as student academic performance and student-teacher ratios.

- **Financial Tools:** This area includes hyperlinks for loan quotes at the Loan Center and homeowners insurance quotes at the Insurance Center. The Credit Report hyperlink offers you quick, inexpensive credit reports. Home Values tells you the selling prices of homes by location, and Salary Comparison helps you determine salary equivalents between two U.S. cities. As shown in Figure 9-5, this area also offers you financial calculators for computing monthly home payments, amortization, and other related figures.

Figure 9-5:   The Yahoo! Real Estate payment calculator.

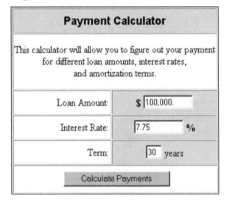

Payment Calculator

This calculator will allow you to figure out your payment for different loan amounts, interest rates, and amortization terms.

Loan Amount:	$ 100,000.
Interest Rate:	7.75 %
Term:	30 years

Calculate Payments

- **Real Estate News:** This area provides hyperlinks to the latest news headlines from Inman News and Real Times.

- **Yellow Pages:** This area provides hyperlinks to agents, appraisal, inspection services, and other resources.

- **Yahoo! Categories:** Hyperlinks are listed for a variety of related topics, including <u>Architecture</u>, <u>Corporate Housing</u>, <u>Relocation Services</u>, <u>Self Storage</u>, and <u>Title Insurance</u>.

- **National Mortgage Rates Averages:** This area posts the nationwide minimum, average, and maximum home loan rates for 30-year fixed, 15-year fixed, and 1-year ARM notes. Clicking the <u>Rates for your region</u> hyperlink tells you rates for U.S. states and for popular metro areas.

- **Yahoo! Loan Center:** This area provides hyperlinks for Custom Mortgage Quotes; Monitor a Mortgage, which lets you compare your current mortgage against market offerings that may be more financially favorable; Mortgage Recommendations, based on your personal financial factors; and Pre-Qualify for a Mortgage.

Listing and Getting Employment Opportunities

Hunting for that perfect new job and posting available employment positions with your company have moved beyond newspaper want ads and careers fairs as their primary communications vehicles. Information exchange regarding career opportunities is now an online venture, and Yahoo! Employment is one of the best places to look for and tell others about jobs.

Access Yahoo! Employment using one of the following methods:

■ At the Yahoo! home page (www.yahoo.com), click the Employment hyperlink in the Other Guides area at the bottom of the page.

■ Type http://employment.yahoo.com into your browser and press Enter or Return.

On the Employment main page, you can find valuable job information on everything from training and development to recruiting and placement to advice on interviewing and negotiating. Here are two of the areas included:

■ **Jobs Quick Search:** As shown in Figure 9-6, this area offers drop-down lists where you can choose a location, choose a job function, and click Find a job! to locate employment matching your criteria. Click any listed job for additional information.

Figure 9-6:   Pick a location, pick a job, and watch as Yahoo! Employment lists your matches.

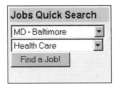

Jobs Quick Search
MD - Baltimore
Health Care
Find a Job!

- **Career Resources:** This area provides a number of hyperlinks to help you in your job search. Click the <u>Post FREE Classifieds</u> hyperlink to list a job opportunity with your organization in the Yahoo! Classifieds.

Travel

Planning and going on a trip has never been easier than with Yahoo! Travel. You can check departure and arrival times for air and ground travel, find the best hotel rates, and peruse itineraries for vacation packages, such as cruises. After you craft the perfect trip, you need only a major credit card to book your reservations and buy your tickets.

Access Yahoo! Travel using one of the following methods:

- At the Yahoo! home page (`www.yahoo.com`), click the <u>Travel</u> hyperlink in the Frequently Accessed Categories area at the top of the page.

- Type `http://travel.yahoo.com` into your browser and press Enter or Return.

Table 9-1 tells you about the resource areas on the main Travel page.

Table 9-1:   Travel Page Areas of Interest

Area	Do This	To Do This
My Trips	Click Current Reservations	See a list of the details of all trips you have booked.
	Click Check Flight Time	Check whether departing and arriving flights are on schedule.
	Click Flight Tracker Pro	Access real-time flight data for aircraft as they fly. Very cool.
Best Fares	Input the destination cities	Receive a constantly updated poll of the cheapest prices on the Web to travel there.
Make Reservations	Enter the date and destination of your trip	Book fares for air, rental car, and hotel — anywhere in the world
Plan Your Trip	Enter a destination in the search box	Hyperlinked information eading to pages with l extensive details about your potential trip

CHAPTER 10

KEEPING TRACK OF YOUR LIFE WITH YAHOO! CALENDAR

IN THIS CHAPTER

- Opening your Yahoo! Calendar

- Adding, editing, and deleting events

- Scheduling reminders

- Changing your view of the Yahoo! Calendar

Yahoo! Calendar is a free, online organizational tool that helps you keep track of your frenetically-busy, Internet-enhanced life. Like standard day planners, you can use it to jot down to-do lists and to record your professional and not-so-professional activities by the hour, day, week, month, and year. But unlike standard planners, you can use Yahoo! Calendar to instantly schedule online events — like chats and Net broadcasts — and send you reminders of upcoming events as they approach.

Accessing the Calendar

You can use Yahoo! Calendar on any computer that has Internet access and a Web browser. For Netscape Navigator and Microsoft Internet Explorer browsers, you must use version 2.0 or higher.

Summon the calendar, as shown in Figure 10-1, in one of three ways:

■ Click the <u>Calendar</u> hyperlink listed among the Frequently Accessed Categories area on the Yahoo! home page.

■ Click the <u>Calendar</u> hyperlink listed on My Front Page if you have customized your page to include the calendar.

■ Type http://calendar.yahoo.com into your browser and press Enter or Return.

Figure 10-1:   The Yahoo! Calendar.

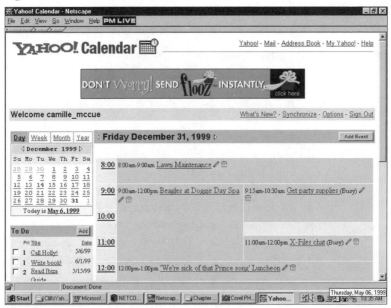

Adding and Editing Events

Adding new events to your calendar involves knowing when the event takes place, sending out online invitations to others who you want to take part in the event, and setting up a reminder to be sent to you as the event approaches. Editing events is simply a matter of opening an event you've already created, making whatever changes you desire, and then saving those changes so that the event automatically updates on your calendar.

Inserting and modifying events in your calendar

Schedule new events or edit existing events in your calendar as follows:

1. Summon the Add Event or Edit Event page to add or edit your event, as follows:

To add a new event: From any view in Yahoo! Calendar, click the Add Event button or the Add hyperlink. Doing so summons the Add Event page (see Figure 10-2).

To edit an existing event: From the Day or Week view in Yahoo! Calendar, click the Pencil icon or click the Edit hyperlink on the event you want to edit. Doing so summons the Edit Event page.

Figure 10-2:   The Add Event page.

2. Type or edit the name of the event in the Event Name box. This name appears on your calendar on the date scheduled for the event.

3. Select the type of event by locating the Type drop-down list box, clicking the arrow, and selecting an event type from the list. Choices include Appointment, Bill Payment, Meeting, Net Event, and others.

4. You can decide how much information to let other people know about your schedule by selecting the Private radio button (this event is no one's business), the Show as Busy radio button (I'm busy but I won't say with what), and the Public radio button (this is what I'm doing). You have to click the publish this calendar hyperlink to make your event public.

5. Select a date for your event by clicking the arrow and selecting a month, day, and year for the event from the Date drop-down list boxes.

6. Select either the All Day Event radio button for an event that takes place on a certain day (such as vacation or someone's birthday) or the Timed Event radio button for events that happen during a particular time. For timed events, you have to supply information in the Start Time and Duration fields, as follows:

Start Time: Click the arrow to select an hour from the drop-down list. Do the same to select the number of minutes past the hour from the drop-down list. Select either the AM or PM radio button.

Duration: Click the arrows to select the number of hours and minutes your event will last from the drop-down lists.

7. If you want, you can type a description of your event in the Description box (you're limited to 100 characters).

8. Click the Save button to add the new event to your calendar, or click the Cancel button to scrap the event.

Invitation

You can send online invitations to other Yahoo!s announcing each event you add or edit in your calendar. Invitation recipients can easily add your announced event to their calendars by pressing the <u>Add to my calendar</u> hyperlink that arrives with your announcement. To send invitations when you add a new event, follow these steps:

1. At the Add Event or Edit Event page, scroll down to the Invitation section.

2. Indicate who you want the invitations delivered to by typing information into the areas described in Table 10-1 (for each, you can click the <u>Address Book</u> hyperlink to select names from your address book).

3. Click the Save button to send the invitation(s), or click Cancel to halt sending them.

Table 10-1: Invitation Fields

Field	What to Type
To	Type the Yahoo! e-mail address for each person you're inviting. You can even invite people outside of Yahoo! Use commas to separate each address in a list of addresses, for example: `Big_Daddy@yahoo.com` or `ScooBDoo@aol.com`.
Cc	Type the Yahoo! e-mail address for each person you want to send a carbon copy of your invitation. Use commas to separate each address in the list.
Bcc	Type the Yahoo! e-mail address for each person you want to send a blind carbon copy of your invitation. (Other people receiving your invitation don't know that you're copying to the Bcc recipients.)

Repeat

For events that occur more than once — weekly *X-Files* chats, monthly pot-luck luncheons, anniversaries — you can set up the Yahoo! Calendar to automatically schedule the events on a repeating basis. Here's how:

1. At the Add Event or Edit Event page, scroll down to the Repeat section.

2. Select a radio button to indicate how you want the schedule of the event repeated:

Do not repeat: The event is a one-shot deal.

Repeat: Choose a frequency and an interval. Frequency choices are Every, Every other, Every third, Every fourth. Interval choices are Day; Week; Month; Year; Mon, Wed, Fri; Tues & Thurs; Mon Thru Fri; and Sat & Sun.

Repeat on the: Select First, Second, Third, Fourth, or Last; choose a day of the week (Sun, Mon, and so on); choose every month, other month, 3 months, 4 months, 6 months, year.

3. Click a radio button to indicate the limits on when the repeating event occurs:

Always: The event has no termination date in sight or, as the song says, until the 12th of Never.

Until: Choose a month, day, and year on which the recurring event terminates.

4. Click the Save button to register the repeat information, or click the Cancel button.

Reminder

Like a wake-up call, a reminder is a friendly nudge letting you know that a scheduled calendar event is about to transpire. You can set one or two reminders, and you can receive each reminder anywhere from five minutes to 14 days prior the event. Follow these steps to send yourself a reminder for a calendar event:

1. At the Add Event or Edit Event page, scroll down to the Reminder section.

2. Complete the information for each area in the Reminder section. See Table 10-2 for your choices.

3. Click the Save button to set up the reminders for delivery, or press Cancel to discard these reminders.

Table 10-2: Areas in the Reminder Section

Area	How to Fill It In
Send a reminder	Click the tab to reveal a drop-down list of times. Choices consist of 5 minutes, 10 minutes, 15 minutes, 30 minutes, 1 hour, 1 day, 2 days, 3 days, . . . up to 14 days. You can also choose a reminder time for the second reminder box.
E-mail	Select the Email check box and then type your Yahoo! e-mail address (camille_mccue@yahoo.com) to have the reminders sent to your e-mail account.
Yahoo! Messenger	Select the Yahoo! Messenger check box. If you already use Yahoo! Messenger, the reminder comes automatically. If you don't yet have a messenger, you need to get one and set up your messenger account. (See Chapter 8 for more information on using the Yahoo! Messenger.)
Mobile device	Check this box and then type an e-mail address that delivers messages to your cellular phone, personal pager, or other mobile device.

Viewing events

To view an event on your calendar, simply click the hyper-linked name of the event (in day or week view). An Event Details page appears, displaying information about your event, such as event type, scheduled time, and duration. For Net Events, the Event Details page may list your event as a hyperlink that, when clicked, connects you to additional event information on another Web page.

The Event Details page also includes an area labeled Want to tell others about this event? To do so:

1. Select the HTML code in the scroll box at the bottom of the Event Details page.

2. Choose Edit⇨Copy.

3. Compose an e-mail message to other persons you want to inform of this event. For more information on using e-mail, see Chapter 5.

4. Click in the body of your email message, and choose Edit⇨Paste to paste the copied URL into the message.

5. Send the e-mail message(s). When recipients click the copied URL, the event appears in their own Yahoo! Calendars.

Adding and Editing To-Dos

Instead of keeping scraps of paper with lists on them or scrawling a note on your hand, Yahoo! Calendar offers you a better alternative: using its To-Do list. You can access your To-Do list from any view in the calendar, and you can add, edit, and delete items as you complete them. You assign a due date and a priority for each, and you can list To-Dos by name, priority, or due date; listing by due date shows the most immediate To-Dos at the top. Here's how to work with To-Dos:

1. Summon the Add To-Do page or the Edit To-Do page to add or edit a To-Do item as follows:

To add a new To-Do item: From any view in Yahoo! Calendar, click the Add button on the To-Do list. Doing so summons the Add To-Do page.

To edit an existing To-Do item: From any view in Yahoo! Calendar, select the To-Do item you want to edit and then click the Edit icon (looks like a pencil) or click the Edit hyperlink at the Event Details page. Doing so summons the Edit To-Do page (see Figure 10-3).

Figure 10-3: The Edit To-Do page.

2. At the Add To-Do or Edit To-Do page, supply or edit the following information for your event:

To-Do Title: Name the To-Do item using no more than 20 characters.

Description: Type details of the To-Do item to help you remember what you're really supposed to do.

Due Date: Click the arrows and select from the drop-down lists a month, day, and year when you must complete your To-Do.

Priority: Choose a priority from the drop-down list: 1 is most important, 5 is "Priority? This isn't a priority!"

Status: Choose Done or Undone.

Sharing: Choose Private or Public, depending on whether you want other Yahoo!s to be privy to the To-Do item.

3. Press the Save button to add or update your To-Do item, or press Cancel.

To mark a To-Do as complete in any view, click the check box next to the item. To remove a completed To-Do from your list, click the Remove Checked button at the bottom of the To-Do list. Completed To-Dos aren't actually deleted — they're just hidden depending on the references you select in Calendar Options.

Deleting Events and To-Dos

Just like scratching off — or whiting out — an activity recorded in your day planner, sometimes you need to delete events and To-Dos from your calendar. Obliterate them by using any of these methods:

■ To delete an event from the Day or Week view in Yahoo! Calendar, click the Trash Can icon or click the <u>Delete</u> hyperlink on the event you want to edit.

■ To delete a To-Do from any view in Yahoo! Calendar, click the name of the To-Do item to summon the Event Details page. Then click the Trash Can icon to delete the To-Do.

■ To delete all events and To-Dos on your entire calendar, click the <u>Options</u> hyperlink at the top of calendar, click <u>Advanced Options</u> ☞ <u>Delete all events and To-Do items from your calendar</u>. Be careful with this action because you can't undo it!

Changing Your View

You can elect to view your calendar using any of four options: by day, week, month, or year. Use the hyperlinks in the upper-left corner of your calendar to switch from one view to another.

If you schedule an event that falls outside your default day view hours, the calendar automatically adds new lines to your day view to include the time of the event.

CLIFFSNOTES REVIEW

Use this CliffsNotes Review to practice what you've learned in this book and to build your confidence in doing the job right the first time. After you work through the review questions, the problem-solving exercises, and the fun and useful practice projects, you're well on your way to achieving your goal of exploring the Internet with Yahoo!.

Q&A

1. To find a sweater that you want to buy in Yahoo!, you should:

   a. Try to find the category that contains clothiers.

   b. Browse in the **Business & Economy** directory.

   c. Browse in the **Regional** directory for Ireland.

2. If you want to locate the Louvre, you should _____ the Yahoo! directories, but if you want to explore museums in general, you should _____ the Yahoo! directories.

3. Before you can personalize My Yahoo!, you have to:

   a. Create a Yahoo! profile.

   b. Sign the My Yahoo! license agreement.

   c. Sign up with Yahoo! to get a Yahoo! ID and password.

4. The first page that you see when you sign in to My Yahoo! is called:

   a. My Personalized Page

   b. My Front Page

   c. My Yahoo! Page

5. To send a copy of an e-mail to someone without the recipient's knowledge, you should

   a. Add the person to the Bcc line.

   b. Add the person to the Cc line.

   c. Click the Reply to All button.

6. You're supposed to pick up a friend who's coming to visit from the airport. Before you leave for the airport, you should

_____

7. The @ symbol at the end of a directory name means:

a. That directory hasn't been approved by Yahoo!.

b. That directory is an alias of the directory's real location.

c. That directory is a bottom-level directory.

8. Which of the following is *not* a way that you can use to remember a Yahoo! Net Event?

a. Record the event in your Yahoo! Calendar.

b. Have Yahoo! send you a reminder e-mail.

c. Have Yahoo! automatically connect you with the Net Event when it starts.

9. What Yahoo! guide or category is especially designed for youngsters?

_____

10. Which of the following is *not* an item you can track using Yahoo! Messenger?

a. Weather

b. Stocks

c. Sports

Answers: (1) b. (2) search, browse (3) c. (4) b. (5) a. (6) Check whether your friend's plane is on time by clicking the Check Flight Time hyperlink at http://travel.yahoo.com. (7) b. (8) c. (9) Yahooligans! (10) a.

Scenario

1. While browsing the Yahoo! directories, you find a site that you may want to go back to in the future. To make this easier, you should _____

2. You want to exchange instant messages with a friend. What do you do to prepare to send messages? _____

_____

_____

3. You have an unusual interest and want to create an area for people who share your interest. To make an area on Yahoo! for people who share your interest, you should _____

_____

_____

Answers: (1) Bookmark the site in your browser. (2) Invite your friend to get the pager program and add the friend to your Friends list. (3) Go to the Clubs Web page and click the <u>Create a Club</u> hyperlink.

CLIFFSNOTES RESOURCE CENTER

The learning doesn't need to stop here. CliffsNotes Resource Center shows you the best of the best — links to the best information in print and online about exploring the Internet. And this isn't all that is available to you; check out www.cliffsnotes.com for more incredibly useful information about Yahoo! and the Internet. Look for all the terrific resources at your favorite bookstore or local library and on the Internet.

Books

This CliffsNotes book is one of many great books about the Internet published by IDG Books Worldwide, Inc. So if you want some great next-step books, check out these other publications:

Teach Yourself the Internet and the World Wide Web VISUALLY. A good next step for someone who learns better by seeing than by reading would be to get this visually stunning book about using the Internet by Maran Graphics. Find out how to use browsers, FTP, chats, and more by looking at pictures similar to what you see on your computer screen. Don't read about where to click your mouse and why — look at it! (IDG Books Worldwide) $29.99

Creating Web Pages For Dummies Quick Reference. After you've nosed around Yahoo!'s directories and gotten a feel for what makes a good Web page, you may want to create a Web page of your own. This book by hilarious *...For Dummies* author Doug Lowe gives you easy-to-understand information on designing, building, and publishing Web pages in a format that makes the information a cinch to find. Now you can submit *your* home page to Yahoo! too! (IDG Books Worldwide, Inc.) $19.99

Digital Photography For Dummies, 2nd Edition. Want to e-mail pictures of your new puppy to a fellow Yahoo! or post them on your Web page? Then this book by Julie Adair King is for you. Find out how to pick a digital camera, touch up your photos on your computer screen, and send the photo to a friend. The book even includes a trial version of Adobe Photoshop, which sets the standard for professional image-editing software. (IDG Books Worldwide, Inc.) $24.99

CliffsNotes Investing Online with Schwab. Almost everyone needs to save and invest more money. If you've been considering joining the online investing revolution, then why not combine two proven winners: Charles Schwab and Cliffs-Notes? Investing expert Kathleen Sindell instructs you on how to obtain an account, plan, research, and buy and sell securities online. (IDG Books Worldwide, Inc.) $8.99

Fantasy Sports Online For Dummies. If you're a sports fan, then you won't be cruising the Internet long before you bump into a fantasy sports contest with *real* prizes. If you want to know how to get started in fantasy sports, where to play, and great strategies to win, pick up this book by Jim Keogh and Gus Nunziata. (IDG Books Worldwide, Inc.) $24.99

Finding books published by IDG Books Worldwide, Inc. is a snap. Check out your favorite bookstore in your town, or go to your favorite online bookseller. You can also check out the following Web sites where the books are available for you to buy:

- `www.dummies.com`
- `www.idgbooks.com`
- `www.cliffsnotes.com`

Internet

Providing next-step sites from Yahoo! (a site that has everything) is certainly a challenge, but I've endeavored to bring you some of the top non-Yahoo! sites on the Internet:

C|NET, `www.cnet.com` Keep up with what's happening in the digital world on this top computer-industry news site.

MP3.com, `www.mp3.com` Download the MP3 player and check out music from bands that may not be tied to major record labels. If you like the sample, you can buy the music online! Cool!

Monster.com, `www.monster.com` Find a better job with the most popular job-searching site on the Internet.

Shareware.com, `www.shareware.com` Looking for a new game or utility? Then check out this site. Search for the kind of program you want, or look through the top downloads list.

Blue Mountain, `www.bluemountain.com` When you forget a birthday or anniversary, point your browser to the most popular online greeting card site.

Geocities, `www.geocities.com` Post a Web page on the Internet for free (as long as you abide by the Geocities guidelines).

The next time you're on the Internet, don't forget to drop by `www.cliffsnotes.com` for a list of great sites like these in much greater depth.

Magazines & Other Media

The following media offerings can help keep you up to date on exploring the world with Yahoo! Most of these magazines can be found at your neighborhood bookstore. And where these magazines publish online, I provide the Web site URL. Usually magazine Web sites offer some information for free, but to get all the available information, you have to subscribe.

The Industry Standard provides those interested in the business of the Internet complete coverage of the people, jobs companies and trends shaping today's Internet economy. (www.thestandard.com) The first four issues are free, and the subscription rate is $49.97 for 40 issues per year.

Wired Magazine provides hip coverage of the online technologies that are transforming our lives. In the words of the publication itself, "It speaks not just to the high-tech professionals and the business savvy, but also to the forward-looking, the culturally astute, and the simply curious. (www.wired.com/wired) The first two issues are free, and the subscription rate is $21.95 for 10 additional issues.

Yahoo! Internet Life is a collaborative publication between Yahoo! and Ziff Davis that keeps you apprised of all the cool — and critically important — developments in the online world. (www.zdnet.com/yil/) The first issue is free, and the subscription rate is $19.99 for 11 additional issues.

Send Us Your Favorite Tips

In your quest for learning, have you ever experienced that sublime moment when you figure out a trick that saves time or trouble? Perhaps you realized you were taking ten steps to accomplish something that could have taken two. Or you've found a little-known workaround that gets great results. If you've discovered a useful tip for using Yahoo! more effectively that you'd like to share, we'd love to hear from you. Go to our Web site at www.cliffsnotes.com and look for the Talk to Us button. If your tip is selected, we may publish it as part of CliffsNotes Daily, our exciting free email newsletter. To find out more, or to subscribe to a newsletter, go to www.cliffsnotes.com on the Web.

INDEX

COMING SOON FROM CLIFFSNOTES

Online Shopping

HTML

Choosing a PC

Beginning Programming

Careers

Windows 98 Home Networking

eBay Online Auctions

PC Upgrade and Repair

Business

Microsoft Word 2000

Microsoft PowerPoint 2000

Finance

Microsoft Outlook 2000

Digital Photography

Palm Computing

Investing

Windows 2000

Online Research

IDG
BOOKS
WORLDWIDE

COMING SOON FROM CLIFFSNOTES
Buying and Selling on eBay

Have you ever experienced the thrill of finding an incredible bargain at a specialty store or been amazed at what people are willing to pay for things that you might toss in the garbage? If so, then you'll want to learn about eBay — the hottest auction site on the Internet. And CliffsNotes *Buying and Selling on eBay* is the shortest distance to eBay proficiency. You'll learn how to:

- Find what you're looking for, from antique toys to classic cars

- Watch the auctions strategically and place bids at the right time

- Sell items online at the eBay site

- Make the items you sell attractive to prospective bidders

- Protect yourself from fraud

Here's an example of how the step-by-step CliffsNotes learning process simplifies placing a bid at eBay:

1. Scroll to the Web page form that is located at the bottom of the page on which the auction item itself is presented.

2. Enter your registered eBay username and password and enter the amount you want to bid. A Web page appears that lets you review your bid before you actually submit it to eBay. After you're satisfied with your bid, click the Place Bid button.

3. Click the Back button on your browser until you return to the auction listing page. Then choose View⇨Reload (Netscape Navigator) or View⇨Refresh (Microsoft Internet Explorer) to reload the Web page information. Your new high bid appears on the Web page, and your name appears as the high bidder.